THE PRESERVATION OF TWO INFANT TEMPERAMENTS INTO ADOLESCENCE

Jerome Kagan, Nancy Snidman, Vali Kahn, and Sara Towsley

WITH COMMENTARY BY
Laurence Steinberg
Nathan A. Fox

W. Andrew Collins
Series Editor

MONOGRAPHS OF THE SOCIETY FOR RESEARCH IN CHILD DEVELOPMENT

Serial No. 287, Vol. 72, No. 2, 2007

Blackwell Publishing   *Boston, Massachusetts   Oxford, United Kingdom*

EDITOR
W. ANDREW COLLINS
University of Minnesota

MANAGING EDITOR
DETRA DAVIS
Society for Research in Child Development

Board of Advisory Editors

Brian K. Barber
University of Tennessee

Glenn I. Roisman
University of Illinois

Michael P. Maratsos
University of Minnesota

Kathleen Thomas
University of Minnesota

Manfred Van Dulmen
Kent State University

Philip David Zelazo
University of Toronto

CONSULTING EDITORS

Mark Appelbaum
University of California, San Diego

William Arsenio
Wesleyan University

Rebecca Bigler
University of Texas-Austin

Peg Burchinal
University of North Carolina Chapel Hill

Susan Campbell
University of Pittsburgh

Stephanie Carlson
University of Washington

W. Andrew Collins
University of Minnesota

Kenneth Dodge
Duke University

William Dukowski
Corcordia University

Nancy Eisenberg
Arizona State University

Nancy Galambos
University of Alberta

Shaun Gallagher
University of Central Florida

Susan Gelman
University of Michigan

Elizabeth Gershoff
Columbia University

Thomas Gould
Temple University

Joan Grusec
University of Toronto

Steven Guberman
University of Colorado

Jeffrey J. Haugaard
Cornell University

R. Peter Hobson
Tavistock Clinic Development psychopathology Research Unit London, England

Tim Ingold
University of Aberdeen, United Kingdom

Andrew Karpinski
Temple University

Robert Larzeler
University of Nebraska

Campbell Leaper
University of California, Santa Cruz

Suniya Luthar
Columbia University

Peter Marshall
Temple University

Robert McCall
University of Pittsburgh

Constance Milbrath
*University of California,
San Francisco*

Lou Moses
University of Oregon

Ulrich Mueller
University of Victoria, Victoria, Canada

Larry Nucci
University of Illinois at Chicago

Sue Parker
Sonoma University

Gregory S. Petit
Auburn University

Glenn I. Roisman
University of Illinois

Paul Quinn
University of Delaware

Karen Saywitz
Harbor UCLA Medical School

Bryan Sokol
Simon Fraser University

Elizabeth Vandewater
*University of Texas,
Austin*

Manfred Van Dulmen
Kent State University

David Wolfe
*Center for Addiction & Mental Health
London,
Ontario, CA*

Hongling Xie
Temple University

THE PRESERVATION OF TWO INFANT TEMPERAMENTS INTO ADOLESCENCE

CONTENTS

ABSTRACT	vii
I. INTRODUCTION	1
II. THE LONGITUDINAL STUDY	10
III. THE CURRENT STUDY	19
IV. RESULTS	31
V. DISCUSSION	44
REFERENCES	61

COMMENTARY

COMMENTARY	
Laurence Steinberg	76
COMMENTARY: FINISHED AND UNFINISHED BUSINESS	
Nathan A. Fox	81
CONTRIBUTORS	92
STATEMENT OF EDITORIAL POLICY	94

ABSTRACT

This *Monograph* reports theoretically relevant behavioral, biological, and self-report assessments of a sample of 14–17-year-olds who had been classified into one of four temperamental groups at 4 months of age. The infant temperamental categories were based on observed behavior to a battery of unfamiliar stimuli. The infants classified as high reactive (20% of the sample) displayed vigorous motor activity and frequent crying. Those classified as low reactives (40%) displayed minimal motor activity and crying. About 25% of the infants, called distressed, showed minimal motor activity but cried frequently, and 10%, characterized by vigorous motoricity but little crying, were called aroused. Evaluations of these children at 14 and 21 months, and 4, 7, and 11 years revealed that the high reactives were most likely to be avoidant of unfamiliar events at the early ages and emotionally subdued, cautious, and wary of new situations at the later ages. By contrast, the low reactives were the least avoidant of unfamiliarity in the second year and most emotionally spontaneous and sociable at the later ages. The participants in the other two groups displayed intermediate profiles. At age 11 years, the high reactives were more likely than the low reactives to display right hemisphere activation in the EEG, a larger evoked potential from the inferior colliculus, larger event related waveforms to discrepant scenes, and greater sympathetic tone in the cardiovascular system.

The current evaluation revealed that, at 14–17 years of age, more high than low reactives were likely to be subdued in unfamiliar situations, to report a dour mood and anxiety over the future, to be more religious, to display sympathetic tone in the cardiovascular system, to combine a fast latency with a large magnitude of the evoked potential from the inferior colliculus, and to show shallower habituation of the event-related potential to discrepant visual events. As at earlier ages, there were low correlations among the biological measures. However, there was stronger dissociation between behavior and biology at age 15 than at earlier ages. Finally, infant temperamental category at 4 months was not a less powerful predictor of behavior at age 15 than the combination of temperament and fearful behavior in the second year.

I. INTRODUCTION

The sense meaning of a temperamental bias is a biologically based foundation for a cluster of feelings and actions appearing during early childhood, although not always in the opening weeks or months, that is sculpted by the environment into a large, but limited, combination of traits that define a personality. Personality traits, such as extraversion, conscientiousness, or impulsivity, are the joint products of a personal history and a temperamental bias (Heinrichs et al., 2006). It is assumed, but not yet proven, that the biological foundations for many, but certainly not all, human temperaments are heritable neurochemical profiles.

GENES, NEUROCHEMISTRY, AND TEMPERAMENT

Research findings over the past few decades have provided a preliminary scaffolding for hypotheses concerning biological bases for some human temperaments. This monograph is concerned primarily with the two infant temperamental biases called high and low reactive. Although the inconclusiveness of the neurochemistry behind these categories precludes a discussion of their possible genetic bases, a select and concise review of existing research relating genes, brain chemistry, and behavior may provide initial clues to the answers we seek.

At least 150 different molecules, along with the density and location of their receptors, potentially influence the emotions and behaviors that define the many human temperaments. These molecules include norepinephrine, dopamine, epinephrine, serotonin, corticotropin-releasing hormone (CRH), glutamate, γ-aminobutyric acid (GABA), opioids, vasopressin, oxytocin, prolactin, monoamine oxidase (MAO), neuropeptide S, and the sex hormones androgen and estrogen (Hartl & Jones, 2005). The genes that represent the origins of these molecules and their receptor distributions often have multiple polymorphisms (i.e., variation in the DNA sequence, sometimes called an allele) in one or more of the gene's exons, introns, or in the regulatory sequences contiguous with the exons, called promoters and enhancers. Promoters control the effectiveness of the transcription of the exon into messenger RNA; enhancers determine where and when the transcription, which will eventuate in amino acids and proteins, will occur. For example, the enhancer region for the gene for neuropeptide P ensures its expression in the central area of the amygdala (Davidson et al., 2006). Recent research has challenged the older concept of a gene as a discrete entity with a particular structure and fixed contributions to a phenotype. Rather, it appears that each gene should be regarded as a flexible entity with borders defined by its location and its responsivity to particular signals (Dillon, 2003). If each gene, consisting of exons, introns, enhancers, and promoters that influenced brain chemistry had five polymorphisms on average, there would be at least 3^{750} possible neurochemical combinations that could contribute to a temperamental bias (Irizarry & Galbraith, 2004). Even if a majority of these neurochemical profiles had no relevance for any temperament, the large number of remaining patterns implies that future scientists will discover many new neurochemical bases for temperaments.

Some Examples

The following are five frequently studied polymorphisms that appear to be significant for some human temperaments: (1) the short (s) and long (l) variants in the promoter region of the gene for the serotonin transporter molecule (5-HTTLPR); between 15% and 20% of most Caucasian samples have the two short forms, whereas 30–40% have the two long forms (Hariri & Brown, 2006; Surtees et al., 2006); (2) presence of the base adenine or guanine in codon 158 of the gene for the enzyme catechol-o-methyltransferase (COMT), which degrades catecholamine transmitters, resulting in either the amino acid valine or methionine (the latter is associated with less COMT activity); (3) the number of repeats of a 48 base pair sequence in the third exon of the gene for the dopamine D4 receptor (DRD4) (the four repeat allele is the most frequent among human populations) (Ding et al., 2002); (4) variation in the DRD4 promoter region; and (5) variation in the promoter region of the gene for MAO (A or B) associated with differential degradation of serotonin, norepinephrine, and epinephrine in the synapse (Hartl & Jones, 2005).

Investigators have reported relations between one or more of these polymorphisms and psychological variables potentially related to the temperamental biases psychologists study. For example, relaxed, compared with irritable, 2-year-olds possessed the longer variant of 5-HTTLPR (Auerbach et al., 1999), and very shy school-age children, as well as prepubertal rhesus monkeys who showed timidity to novelty, had the two short forms of 5-HTTLPR (Battaglia et al., 2005; Bethea et al., 2004).

Further, the serotonin transporter gene was less active in the amygdala of depressed adults (Parsey et al., 2006b) and in the raphe nucleus of female cynomolgus monkeys who were prone to stress (Bethea et al., 2005).

Further evidence has come from research on the seven repeat variant of the DRD4 gene. This gene was more common among: (1) 1-year-old Israeli infants who showed less sustained attention to objects in a play situation (Auerbach et al., 2001); (2) Italian 3-year-olds who were intense in their reaction to novelty (DeLuca et al., 2003); and (3) heroin addicts (Kotler et al., 1997). In studies with adults, Polish women with panic disorder were more likely to have four or more repeats in the promoter region of the MAO A gene (Samochowiec et al., 2004); whereas European men who used violent means in an attempted suicide, compared with those who used nonviolent methods, were more likely to have fewer repeats (two to three repeats) in this region (Courtet et al., 2005).

Because brain states are the products of reciprocal interactions among many molecules, many psychological phenotypes should be the product of combinations of polymorphisms. For example, oxytocin potentiates the secretion of norepinephrine to a novel event (Pfister & Muir, 1989), vasopressin is suppressive of norepinephrine secretion (Onaka & Yagi, 1993), and androgen modulates the consequences of norepinephrine release following exposure to novelty (Handa et al., 1994; Kerr, Beck, & Handa, 1996; Hanson, Jones, & Watson, 2004).

Combinations of polymorphisms have been implicated in the number and variety of behaviors. One-year-olds who showed extreme levels of avoidant behavior to a stranger possessed both the two short alleles of 5-HTTLPR, as well as the seven repeat polymorphism of DRD4, whereas the least avoidant children combined the two long forms of 5-HTTLPR with the seven repeat polymorphism (Lakatos et al., 2003). In adults from a much larger sample a small proportion of individuals who had very high scores on a measure of novelty seeking combined one or both of the long forms of 5-HTTLPR, valine rather than methionine in the amino acid codon of the COMT gene, and seven repeats in the DRD4 gene (Benjamin et al., 2000). Hungarian adults who had high scores on a measure of harm avoidance possessed the two short forms of 5-HTTLPR and the seven repeat of DRD4 (Szekely et al., 2004). Caucasian college women who reported binge drinking were more likely to have the two short alleles of 5-HTTLPR and an allele of MAO A associated with greater expression of the gene (Herman et al., 2005). In one investigation, the combined effects of 19 different brain molecules were required in order to account for 60% of the variation in avoidant behavior in a sample of rats (Ray, Hansen, & Waters, 2006). It is likely that inconsistencies across studies in the reported relations between genes and psychological variables may reflect the common strategy of measuring only one polymorphism, rather than several (Arbelle et al., 2003).

THE INTERACTION WITH EXPERIENCE

Environmental influence is apparent from a growing body of studies documenting interactions between genes and experience. For example, upper-middle-class adults with two or five, rather than seven, repeats of the gene for the DRD4 receptor were high on novelty seeking, but those from economically disadvantaged backgrounds with two or five repeats were not (Lahti et al., 2006). Three different research groups have reported that adolescents who combined one or both of the two short alleles of 5-HTTLPR with lifetime experiences characterized by poverty and stress were more likely than others to report a depressed mood (Caspi et al., 2003; Eley et al., 2004; Kaufman et al., 2004). This finding was not replicated, however, in a much larger sample from a different cultural background (Surtees et al., 2006).

Related evidence showed that young adults characterized by a combination of a harsh childhood environment and a shorter number of repeats, and therefore less activity, in the MAO A allele were most likely to display asocial behavior (Caspi et al., 2002). Similarly, adolescent boys with the shorter number of repeats (three repeats) in the promoter region for MAO A showed asocial characteristics if they also had experienced a high-risk rearing environment (maltreatment and an economically stressed family), whereas adolescent boys with the shorter number of repeats who came from economically advantaged homes had the lowest criminality scores (Nilsson et al., 2005). The combination of a disadvantaged background and maltreatment, which are psychological variables, was a more significant predictor of self-rated criminality than the MAO polymorphism. The presence of the short allele of 5-HTTLPR explained only 2% of the variance in the self-reported distress of a large sample of German adults between 20 and 80 years of age; the distress scores were best predicted by a combination of gender (women more than men) and employment (unemployed more than employed) (Grabe et al., 2005). Thus, investigators trying to predict criminality, depression, or psychic distress would do far better to rely on demographic features than genetic markers alone, even though the combination of genetic markers and psychological features predicts criminality or depression with greater accuracy for a small group. Because historical events alter the prevalence of poverty and childhood abuse within a society, the relation between genes and a specific psychological outcome should vary across time and culture. Thus, current evidence relating genetic variation to psychological phenomena implies that the inconsistent results across studies is probably due to interactions among the diverse physiological products of genes, interactions with experience, and the fact that the relations often vary with the ethnicity, social class, gender, and cultural background of the participants (Manuck et al., 2004).

OTHER CONTRIBUTING FACTORS

Nonheritable alterations in brain chemistry also may account for some neurochemical profiles that influence temperament. For example, a female fetus lying next to her fraternal twin brother is affected by the androgen secreted by the latter and is likely, as an older child, to have a higher pain threshold (Morley-Fletcher et al., 2003). Another example is the modest association between season of conception with behaviors and moods that could be derivatives of a temperament. Early fall conceptions in the Northern Hemisphere (and conceptions in February through April in the Southern Hemisphere) are associated with extreme shyness in children (Gortmaker et al., 1997), an affective disorder (Pjrek et al., 2004; Torrey et al., 1997; Minoshima & Okagami, 2000; Joiner et al., 2002; Hare, 1975), and differential dopamine turnover in the brain (Chotai & Adolfsson, 2002; Chotai et al., 2003). By contrast, spring conceptions in the United States predict illicit drug use (Goldberg & Newlin, 2000) and reports of maximal alertness in the morning rather than the evening (Caci, Robert, Dossios, & Boyer, 2005). It is interesting that the few clinically depressed adolescents in the sample to be described in this monograph were most likely to have been conceived in August or September and none was conceived during the spring months.

Melatonin, secreted by the pineal gland, is a likely contributor to these correlations. All humans secrete larger amounts of melatonin when the hours of daylight are decreasing. Hence, it is not surprising that 8-week-old infants who had been conceived in October had the highest concentration of melatonin metabolites in their urine (Sivan et al., 2001). A pregnant mother's secretion of high levels of melatonin can affect fetal brain development in diverse ways. This molecule binds to receptors in many sites, including the hypothalamus (Thomas et al., 2002), contributes to cell death (Ciesla, 2001), and suppresses both dopamine release (Zisapel, 2001) and cortisol production (Torres-Farton et al., 2004). Hence, it is conceivable that a fetus's genetic vulnerability to a specific temperamental bias could be potentiated by a conception that occurred during the months when the hours of daylight were decreasing.

Summary Comment

If each gene that contributes to a temperamental bias is regarded as a word in a long sentence whose letters could be rearranged (analogous to a polymorphism), and the meaning of the sentence is analogous to a temperament, there are many opportunities for a rearrangement to change the meaning of the sentence. Some alterations, such as "ran" for "run" will have little effect on meaning, but spelling "hate" as "mate" or "rape" as "race" would change meaning more seriously. If a printer had changed "fear" to "tears" or "years" in T. S. Eliot's poetic line, "I'll show you fear in a handful of dust," reader comprehension would have been altered dramatically. Because laboratory assays exist only for a small proportion of the large number of possible polymorphisms (D'Souza & Craig, 2006); however, it is likely that when investigators can measure more of the alleles that affect mood or behavior they will discover that combinations of genes and rearing environments are always the best predictors of the psychological variations that define human temperaments and accompanying personalities.

The immaturity of our current understanding of the relations among genes, brain chemistry, experience, and behavior frustrates any attempt to posit a robust relation between a particular gene or physiological profile and a temperamental bias. As a result, every current definition of a temperament is based on behavior, observed directly, or described by an informant, or self-report questionnaires. Although future investigators will add biological measures to these behaviors when they define a temperamental bias, a psychological component will always be part of the definition because temperament is a psychobiological concept.

REACTION TO UNFAMILIARITY

The central nervous system of every animal is exquisitely sensitive to change. Tiny hairs on the posterior appendage of a cockroach are sensitive to subtle perturbations in air flow (Rinberg & Davidowitz, 2000). Even the tiny nemotode worm (C-elegans), with only 302 neurons, displays a reflex withdrawal if the plate in which it rests is tapped (Rankin, 2000). The infant's cry to the approach of a stranger, one of the first reliable signs of fear to unexpected or novel events, appears long before children experience a fear of failure, attack, domination, spiders, or loss of status.

The simplest unexpected event perturbs the chemistry of the genes within neurons. For example, a novel sound provokes production of the protein c-fos in the rat's cochlear nucleus (Kandiel, Chen, & Hillman, 1999); a novel location provokes production of the CREB molecule (which regulates the synthesis of proteins necessary for creating long-term memories) in the hippocampus (Moncada & Viola, 2006). The novelty of an event can, on occasion, be as important as its hedonic quality. The magnitude of increase in CRH within the central nucleus of the rat amygdala, which usually occurs following stress, is equally large when rats are unexpectedly restrained, which they do not like, but, also, when they are unexpectedly fed (Merali et al., 1998).

INTRODUCTION

The brain states created by unexpected events that are quickly assimilated (e.g., the sound of thunder on a sunny day) and unexpected events that are unfamiliar and thus not easily assimilated (e.g., high-pitched sounds from the fireplace) differ within the first 300 ms. It is also important to distinguish between the state created by an unfamiliar event and the state produced by a familiar event that has become associated with a strong emotion; neuropeptide S contributes to the former but not to the latter (Reinscheid & Xu, 2005). On some occasions, unfamiliar events facilitate recognition memory more effectively than familiar, highly arousing experiences (Izquierdo, 1987).

The unfamiliarity or unexpectedness of an event always depends on the context. Although faces with fearful expressions usually activate the human amygdala, when fear faces were presented along with scenes representing fearful events, the latter, but not the former, activated the amygdala because they were less salient when presented together with the scenes (Schafer, Schienle, & Vaitl, 2005). Similarly, a schematic face with a fearful expression usually evokes a larger ERP waveform than a schematic face with a neutral expression, but presenting the schematic fearful face together with a photograph of a fearful face reduces the power of the former to evoke the waveform (Holmes, Winston, & Eimer, 2005). The approach of a stranger is more likely to produce a cry in 8-month-olds if the setting is an unfamiliar laboratory room rather than the infant's familiar living room. There are few consistent consequences of any foreground event, only consequences of events in specific contexts.

INHIBITED AND UNINHIBITED CHILDREN

Two extensively studied temperamental biases in children older than 1 year are defined by the contrast between a restrained, cautious, or avoidant reaction to unfamiliar persons, objects, events, or places—called inhibited—and a spontaneous approach, called uninhibited (Asendorpf, 1989, 1991; Bates, 1989). There are good reasons to study the behavioral reactions to unfamiliarity. These responses are moderately stable over time, relatively easy to measure, and display variation within every animal species studied (Jones, Hou, & Cook, 1996; Kitchigina, Vankov, Harley, & Sara, 1997; Momozawa et al., 2005; Sara, Dyon-Laurent, & Herve, 1995; Schneirla, 1959; Scott & Fuller, 1965; Wirtshafter, 2005).

The behaviors defining the concepts inhibited and uninhibited to the unfamiliar, first introduced almost 20 years ago, were moderately stable from the second to the fifth year and modestly associated with peripheral biological measurements in theoretical accord with the presumed physiological bases for the two temperaments (Kagan, Reznick, & Snidman, 1988). That is, middle-class, Caucasian 2-year-olds who showed consistent avoidance of, or distress to, unfamiliar people, procedures, and situations—which was the original definition of the concept inhibited—preserved some form of these tendencies over the next few years, along with greater sympathetic tone in the cardiovascular system. By contrast, the uninhibited 2-year-olds displayed minimal avoidance of the unfamiliar and greater parasympathetic tone.

The features that define inhibited and uninhibited behavior to the unfamiliar appear to be heritable. Identical twins have been found to be more similar in displays of inhibited or uninhibited behavior during early childhood than fraternal twins (Bartels et al., 2004; Goldsmith, Lemery, & Buss, 1999; Di Lalla, Kagan, & Reznick, 1994; Kagan & Saudino, 2001; Matheny, 1990). Research findings have found inhibited children to be more likely to be born to families in which one or both parents have an anxiety disorder (Merikangas, Lieb, Wittchen, & Avenevoli, 2003; Rosenbaum et al., 1991), and inhibited children who had a parent diagnosed with panic disorder were likely to have a distinct polymorphism in a region of the CRH gene (Smoller et al., 2005). However, heritability estimates based on equations that assume additivity of the variance associated with genetic and environmental influences are often inflated because the variance allocated to genes represents the combined influences of genes and the interactions between genes and experience. This claim is supported by evidence showing that the heritability values for several salient behaviors characteristic of five dog pedigrees bred especially for hunting were lower than the values reported for most human personality traits; the former were typically <0.4 and some were <0.1 (Schmutz & Schmutz, 1998). It is unlikely that human personality dimensions are more heritable than the behaviors of varied dog strains bred for hunting.

Other research has documented the modest preservation of variation in the psychological reaction to unfamiliarity. For example, teacher ratings of fearfulness from kindergarten through the sixth grade in a group of more than 1,800 Canadian children (Cote et al., 2002) showed modest stability. Boys described by their mothers as very shy during late childhood married, became parents, and established a career later than their less shy peers. Similarly, although very shy girls married at normative times, they were less apt to develop a career and likely to terminate their job once they had married or had a child and to conform to the traditional sex role norms for that historical era (Caspi, Elder, & Bem, 1988; see, also, Kerr, Lambert, & Bem, 1996). Similar reports of stability were found in a sample of more than 1,000 children growing up in New Zealand (Caspi & Silva, 1995).

With respect to relations with age mates, Rubin, Burgess, and Hastings (2002) distinguish between children in peer groups who play alone, stare at other children, and show behavioral signs of timidity (called reticent) and children who also play alone but display no signs of anxiety (called solitary passive). Both types appear to be stable over time, but the former resemble the children we call inhibited (Coplan, Rubin, Fox, Calkins, & Stuart, 1994). Evidence of modest preservation of reticent behavior was also reported for German (Asendorpf, 1991) and Swedish children (Broberg, Lamb, & Hwang, 1990).

Environmental Influences

Shy, reticent behavior also is subject to environmental influences, however. Two-year-olds who were reticent in a laboratory setting preserved that behavioral style only if they also had intrusive, protective, hypercritical mothers. The reticent 2-year-olds were likely to become more sociable over time if their mothers were less protective and discouraged shy behavior (Rubin, Burgess, & Hastings, 2002). Placement in daycare before the second birthday can also reduce the preservation of shy behavior (Fox, Henderson, Rubin, Calkins, & Schmidt, 2001), although the effect of daycare depends on the child's typical behavior pattern. Young infants described by their mothers as distressed by, and reactive to, novelty were more likely to have internalizing symptoms at $2\frac{1}{2}$ years if they spent many hours in out-of-home care, rather than being raised only at home (Crockenberg & Leerkes, 2005).

Despite the evidence of individual and proximal environmental influences, culture, social class, and historical era are among the most important determinants of the behaviors that define a persona of traits and emotional displays. For example, the proportion of children in the United Arab Emirates who are quiet and subdued is greater than the proportion found in most American cities (Eapen et al., 2005). A survey of more than 1,400 Americans revealed that, among women with one or more children, reports of anxiety, sadness, or anger were most frequent for those who did not have a college education (Simm & Nath, 2004). The best predictors of depression and anxiety in American 10-year-olds were membership in a poor, ethnic minority and rearing by a depressed mother who used marijuana during her pregnancy (Leech et al., 2006). Thus, temperamental biases tweak the more important influences of culture, class, and historical era and have their greatest effect on behavior and mood for individuals who live in a particular culture-time warp. As an example, variation in timid or bold behavior among Caucasian children in contemporary middle-class American homes should reflect their temperaments because ethnicity, culture, and historical moment have been controlled. This conclusion does not imply, however, that variation in experiences at home, in school, or with peers are unimportant.

II. THE LONGITUDINAL STUDY

Because our initial assessments of temperamental differences occurred in the second year of life, there was sufficient time for experiences to create the behaviors that define inhibited and uninhibited behavior. For that reason, our laboratory initiated a longitudinal study of a large sample of 16-week-old, Caucasian, middle-class infants with the explicit aim of discovering behaviors that might predict the inhibited and uninhibited profiles, but were unlikely to be the sole product of experience (Kagan, 1994). We theorized that the behavioral reactions to unfamiliar events in older children and adults are the result of three independent factors: the social categories to which individuals believe they belong (e.g., gender, class, ethnicity), the familiarity and social structure of the local context, and temperamental biases. Sixteen-week-old infants are unaware of their social categories and are relatively indifferent to the context in which they are observed. Hence, their behavioral responses to unfamiliar stimuli are governed primarily, but not completely, by temperament.

INFLUENCE OF THE AMYGDALA

The central hypothesis that guided the infant assessments and the analyses of data were that variation in the excitability of the amygdala and its projections to other brain sites and motor and autonomic targets represented an important basis for the later development of inhibited and uninhibited profiles. This hypothesis does not exclude the likely possibility that other brain circuits are also important. The amygdala consists of a number of neuronal clusters—basolateral, cortical, medial, and central areas—each with distinct profiles of connectivity, neurochemistry, and function. The first two clusters, which evolved later than the latter two, establish associations between stimuli and are closely connected to sites in the cerebral cortex. The central and medial areas mediate more automatic, defensive reactions and are more closely connected to the bed nucleus and hypothalamus (McDonald, 2003).

Each cluster within the amygdala projects to at least 15 different sites and receives input from about the same number of regions, resulting in about 600 known amygdalar connections (Petrovich, Centeras, & Swanson, 2001; Stefanacci & Amaral, 2002). Each cluster is differentially sensitive to varied aspects of an event. Some neuronal clusters are sensitive to the physical features of a stimulus (e.g., contour contrast); others to its unfamiliarity; still others to its hedonic valence (e.g., a sweet liquid or a bitter taste) (Holland & Gallagher, 2004; Rolls et al., 2005). The threshold of excitability in the various amygdalar clusters is influenced by a large number of molecules; some are excitatory and some inhibitory. These molecules include GABA, glutamate, opioids, CREB, norepinephrine, dopamine, vasopressin, and oxytocin (Adamec, Blundell, & Burton, 2005a, b; Kirsch et al., 2005). The balance among the molecules will determine the neural state within the components of this structure.

Unfamiliar or unexpected events, whether appetitive or aversive, activate the neurons of the basolateral area of the amygdala which establishes a link between a conditioned stimulus and a salient, unconditioned event. The projections from the central nucleus, which receives input from the basolateral nucleus, can lead to immobility, defensive behavior, increased sympathetic activity, and activation of the HPA axis (Stark et al., 2005; Meller & Dennis, 1991), as well as increased power in the high-frequency γ band of the EEG (Jung et al., 2005).

An amygdalar reaction is not restricted to events that represent a threat of harm or danger (Fitzgerald et al., 2006). For example, some neurons in the monkey amygdala respond to a visual stimulus that signals a desirable liquid reward, whereas other neurons respond to a stimulus signaling an aversive air puff (Paton et al., 2006). Direct recordings from a large number of amygdalar neurons in monkeys watching brief video clips of three actor monkeys displaying either a threat face, a coo face, or a scream face revealed that the facial configuration of one actor emitting a coo call—which has a pleasant valence—generated greater activity in some amygdalar neurons than the face of the same monkey displaying a scream expression associated with fear (Kuraoka & Nakamura, 2006).

Amygdala and Reactivity in Infancy

There is indirect support for the suggestion that a young infant with an excitable amygdala is likely to display inhibited behavior several years later. Newborn infants whose rate of sucking increased dramatically following an unexpected change in taste sensation from water to a sweet substance were markedly more inhibited in the second year than newborns who showed a minimal increase in sucking rate following the same change in taste (LaGasse, Gruber, & Lipsitt, 1989). The unexpected change in taste would have activated the central nucleus of the amygdala, through projections from gustatory receptors to the brainstem and thence to the amygdala, which would be followed by activation of the motor centers that control sucking (Barot & Bernstein, 2005; Koh, Wilkins, & Bernstein, 2003). Infants with a more excitable central nucleus of the amygdala should have displayed a greater increase in sucking rate compared to infants with a less excitable central nucleus.

In many mammalian species activation of the amygdala is followed by limb movements mediated by projections from the basolateral nucleus to the ventral striatum and ventral pallidum; arching of the back mediated by projections from the central nucleus to the central gray; and distress cries, mediated, in part, by projections from the central nucleus to the nucleus ambiguus (Pitkanen, 2000). These data imply that young infants who inherited a neurochemistry that rendered one or more areas of the amygdala excitable should display more vigorous motor activity, especially arches of the back, and more frequent crying to unfamiliar or highly stimulating events, compared with infants who had a neurochemistry that rendered the amygdalar clusters less excitable.

This hypothesis is in accord with Rothbart's (1989) emphasis on variation in reactivity as a temperamental quality in infants. It also appears consistent with varied findings of greater motor tension among high reactives. For example, high levels of muscle tension in the head, neck, and limbs have been found to occur more often in individuals with high levels of uncertainty (Fridlund, Hatfield, Cottam, & Fowler, 1986; Hoehn-Saric, Hazlett, Pourmetabbed, & McLeod, 1997; Wasserman et al., 2001). Among college students who lived together for a semester in 10 member groups, relative perception of power was associated with a relaxed, open-body posture combined with frequent talking (Cashdan, 1998). Evidence from baboons has shown that when a female olive baboon is resting within 5 m of a dominant, compared with a subordinate, animal she makes self-directed motor responses (e.g., scratching, grooming, touching, and shaking) (Castles, Whiten, & Aureli, 1999). The greater motor tension among high reactives could be an indirect consequence of amygdalar projections to the central gray and/or the ventral striatum.

Although the amygdala is the proximal cause of increased motor activity and distress in infants, other neural structures also may be implicated in this connection. Unexpected events activate the locus ceruleus in the brainstem and in turn sends norepinephrine projections to the hippocampus and amygdala. Further, the hippocampus and the perirhinal cortex, which are reciprocally connected to the amygdala, are also activated by novel events (Strange et al., 2005). Therefore, the inherent excitability of the hippocampus, parahippocampal, perirhinal, or entorhinal cortices could be sources of variation in motor activity and crying to unfamiliar or unexpected events (Fried, MacDonald, & Wilson, 1997; Witter et al., 2000). In addition, sites in the anterior cingulate and orbitofrontal prefrontal cortex modulate the amygdala and the behavioral and biological reactions to unfamiliarity (Fischer et al., 1998; Johanson et al., 1998; Kent et al., 2005). It should be noted, however, that this modulating circuit originates in the prefrontal cortex, which is not fully mature at 4 months of age. Although we propose that amygdalar activity participates in the complex circuit responsible for the variation in the motor and distress behaviors that define high and low reactive infants, we do not argue that the excitability of this structure is the only basis for these defining properties. Future research will have to clarify this important issue.

SELECTION OF HIGH AND LOW REACTIVE INFANTS

The behaviors of more than 500 healthy, 16-week-old, Caucasian, middle-class infants, born at term, were filmed while they were presented with unfamiliar visual, auditory, and olfactory stimuli. We quantified limb movement, arching of the back, fretting, crying, vocalization, smiling, and heart rate during the 45-minute battery (see Kagan, 1994, for details). Briefly, the mother initially looked down at her infant smiling but not talking for 1 minute and then went to a chair behind the infant in order to be outside the infant's field of vision. The examiner then placed a speaker baffle to the right of the infant and turned on a tape recorder that played eight short sentences read by a blending of male and female voices. Most infants became quiet and remained alert; a minority of infants thrashed their limbs and cried.

The speaker baffle was removed and the examiner, standing in back of the infant, presented a set of mobiles composed of one, three, or seven unfamiliar colorful toys that moved back and forth slowly in front of the infant's face for 9-, 20-second trials. The examiner then dipped a cotton swab into water or very dilute butyl alcohol and presented it close to the infant's nostrils for eight trials (the first and last trials were water). The speaker baffle was replaced and the infant heard a female voice speaking three nonsense syllables (ma, pa, ga) at three loudness levels. Finally, the mother returned to gaze at her infant for the final minute.

About 20% of the sample displayed qualitatively higher levels of motor activity (limb movement and arches of the back) and crying during the stimulus presentations than the remainder of the sample. These infants, called *high reactive*, were more likely than the remaining infants to display facial expressions indicative of a state of distress (e.g., frowns, pained expressions), and to cry to the onset of a taped human voice. We believe that these reactions are not conditioned responses but reflect the inherent excitability of the central area of the amygdala. By contrast, the 40% of infants who showed minimal motor activity, very few arches, and little crying were classified as *low reactive*. The remaining infants—about 40%—were assigned to one of two other groups (high motor activity with minimal crying or low motor activity with frequent crying) (Kagan, 1994).

The decision to define discrete groups based on the combination of motor activity and crying, rather than a continuum of reactivity, was supported by a taxonomic analysis of the 4-month data. The results of this analysis implied that the combination of the two variables fit a categorical conception better than a continuous one (Woodward et al., 2000). The finding is also in accord with the fact that very high levels of motor activity, which usually involve frequent arches of the back, are mediated by projections from the central nucleus of the amygdala to the central gray. By contrast, less vigorous movements of the arms and legs, without any arching of the back, are mediated by projections from the basolateral nucleus to the ventral striatum. Thus, very high levels of motor activity combined with crying are likely to be the result of different neurochemistries than low levels of motor activity and minimal crying. There may be ethnic differences in the prevalence of these two biases. The proportion of infants classified as high reactive was significantly smaller, and that of low reactives higher, in Chinese 4-month-old born in Beijing than in Caucasian-American (Boston) or Irish samples (Dublin) administered the same battery (Kagan et al., 1994).

Longitudinal Evaluations

Most of these infants ($N = 468$) were evaluated in the laboratory at 14 and 21 months. Fewer children were assessed at 4, $5\frac{1}{2}$, and $7\frac{1}{2}$ years. At 11 years of age, children ($N = 237$) were evaluated. These latter data, summarized in Kagan and Snidman (2004), revealed modest preservation of inhibited behavior among high reactives and uninhibited behavior among low reactives. For example, high reactives were significantly more avoidant of unfamiliar objects and people during the second year, whereas low reactives were more sociable, showed more frequent smiling, engaged laboratory tasks with enthusiasm (Kagan, 1994), and resembled the 3-year-old children classified as extraverted (Olino et al., 2005). Marshall and Fox (2005) have reported that high reactives are most likely to show a pattern of distress during episodes of the Strange Situation that fit the insecure attachment categories called B3-C2 because they cried intensely to maternal departure and were not easily soothed when the mother returned.

BIOLOGICAL MEASURES AT AGE 11

Measures of four biological variables that indirectly reflect the excitability of the amygdala were administered to the 237 children seen at 11 years of age: asymmetry of activation in the EEG; size of Wave 5 response; event-related potential (ERP); and cardiovascular activity. These variables, or variations on them, were also measured on the sample described in this monograph (see Kagan & Snidman, 2004 for details).

Asymmetry of Activation in the EEG

The EEG represents the synchronized activity of large numbers of cortical pyramidal neurons, which, at any moment, have a dominant frequency of oscillation at particular sites. There are usually slight hemispheric differences in the amount of α power (8–13 Hz) at frontal and parietal sites. Because α frequencies are associated with a relaxed psychological state and higher frequencies with a vigilant state, the less α power at a particular site, the more active the neurons at that site (Smit, Eling, & Coenen, 2004). The technical terms for the loss of α power is desynchronization. Increased desynchronization of α frequencies is a sign that the individual has moved from a relaxed to a more aroused state; that is, the site is activated. Left hemisphere activation is more likely when the individual is in a happy or relaxed state. Individuals with greater activation in the left frontal area more often report sanguine moods, are biased to detect pleasant features in pairs of words, and show less anxiety than the smaller proportion who show greater activation in the right frontal area (Davidson, 2003; Davidson, Jackson, & Kalin, 2000; Fox, Calkins, & Bell, 1994; Fox et al., 2005; Schmidt et al., 1999; Sutton & Davidson, 2000). Adults viewing an emotionally arousing aversive film in the left visual field (i.e., with the right hemisphere) show greater increases in blood pressure and secrete more cortisol than when they view the same film in the right visual field (with the left hemisphere), despite no difference in subjective feeling between viewing the films in the right or the left visual field (Wittling & Pfluger, 1990). Six-month-old infants who had responded to the unfamiliarity of a laboratory setting with increased cortisol also showed greater right, than left, frontal activation and displayed a sad facial expression to the approach of a stranger (Buss et al., 2003). Administration of cortisol to adults produced right hemisphere activation (Tops et al., 2005).

However, there are exceptions to these generalizations (Vuga et al., 2006). Because the amygdala projects ipsilaterally, via the nucleus basalis, to the frontal cortex, greater activity in the right amygdala should lead to greater EEG activation in the right frontal area (Cameron, 2002; McLin, Miasnikov, & Weinberger, 2002). Further, visceral feedback from the body to the central nucleus of the amygdala is greater to the right, than to the left, amygdala (Pauli, Wiedemann, & Nickola, 1999; Wittling, 1995), and the right amygdala of rats becomes more activated than the left following exposure to a cat (Adamec, Blundell, & Burton, 2005a). Therefore, children who experience greater visceral activity, either spontaneously or in response to an unfamiliar event, should have a more active right amygdala and display right, rather than left, frontal activation. It should be noted that right versus left frontal activation reflects both a moderately stable trait as well as a transient state (Schmidt et al., 2003; Hagemann et al., 2002, 2005; Vuga et al., 2006). In a group of adults evaluated on three different occasions, measures of asymmetry of EEG activation revealed that 40% of the variance related to greater left or right activation represented a stable trait, whereas about 60% reflected a transient state (Hagemann et al., 2005). Further, asymmetry of activation appears to be less heritable than the amount of power in the α band (Anokhin, Heath, & Myers, 2006).

The 11-year-olds, who had been high, compared with low, reactive as infants had greater activation in the right relative to the left parietal lobe. Further, the high reactives who had been inhibited in the second year showed greater right than left hemisphere activation in both frontal and parietal sites. These data are consistent with evidence reported by Davidson (2003), Fox, Calkins, and Bell (1994), Schmidt, Fox, Schulkin, and Gold (1999), and Wiedemann et al. (1999).

Wave 5

The brainstem auditory evoked response (BAER), which consists of a number of waveforms, is usually measured by administering a series of clicks through earphones over a 1- or 2-minute interval. The magnitude of the fifth positive waveform in the BAER, called Wave 5 and usually quantified as the difference in amplitude between the trough of Wave 3 and the peak of Wave 5, has a latency between 5.5 and 6.0 ms and is believed to reflect the neuronal activity generated by termination of the fibers of the lateral lemniscus on the inferior colliculus (Chiappa, 1983). Because the neurons of the inferior colliculus are primed by the amygdala, a more excitable amygdala should be accompanied by a larger Wave 5 (Brandao, Coimbra, & Osaki, 2001; Marsh et al., 2002; Perez-Gonzalez, Malmierca, & Covey, 2005). The 11-year-olds who had been high reactive as infants displayed a significantly larger Wave 5 than those who had been low reactive. This finding is consistent with evidence that adults displayed a larger Wave 5 when they believed they might receive electric shock than during safe intervals when they knew no shock would be delivered (Baas et al., 2006).

ERP

The third measurement at age 11 years was the magnitude of the ERP to discrepant scenes. The ERP is a time-locked post-synaptic potential generated by large numbers of cortical neurons to a stimulus. The waveforms called P300 and N400, evoked by unexpected or unfamiliar visual events when individuals have no cognitive task to perform, usually appear between 250 and 800 ms primarily at frontal sites. The N400 waveform, which usually appears between 350 and 800 ms, with a mean latency of 400 ms at central and frontal sites, also occurs to the final word in a sentence that renders it semantically inconsistent (e.g., "Carrots are good things to breed") (Federmeier & Kutas, 2002). Studies with monkeys have documented that neurons in the monkey's basolateral nucleus and orbitofrontal prefrontal cortex respond to unfamiliar events and habituate with repeated exposure (Ono & Nishijo, 2000; Rolls et al., 2005). Human young adults who had been classified as inhibited in the second year sustained greater amygdalar activity (as measured by fMRI) to the repeated presentation of unfamiliar, compared with familiar, faces (all with neutral expressions) than adults who had been uninhibited in the second year (Schwartz et al., 2003).

Reciprocal connections between the basolateral nucleus of the amygdala and the locus ceruleus and ventral tegmentum should be accompanied by increased cortical concentrations of norepinephrine and dopamine and, therefore, enhanced synchronization of cortical pyramidal neurons. In addition, the central nucleus of the amygdala projects to the thalamus, which, in turn, projects to cortical neurons. These mechanisms imply larger ERP waveforms to discrepant or unfamiliar events than to familiar or expected ones (Aston-Jones & Bloom, 1981).

The 11-year-olds were presented, through goggles, two series of paired identical chromatic scenes with 169 pictures in each series. In the first series, 70% of the pictures were identical (a fireworks display); 15% were of the same flower (the oddball stimulus), and the remaining 15% were different, but ecologically valid. In the second series the frequent picture presented 70% of the time was a yellow fire hydrant; the oddball stimulus was of a very different flower; and the remaining 15% were unique, but each was ecologically invalid (a chair with three legs, a baby's head on an adult body). The 11-year-olds simply looked at each picture with no task to perform. The high, compared with the low, reactives showed a larger ERP waveform at frontal sites to the invalid scenes.

Cardiovascular System

The fourth set of measurements consisted of indicators sympathetic and parasympathetic tone within the cardiovascular system. Cardiovascular activity is influenced by many brain sites, including the central nucleus of the amygdala, parabrachial nucleus, and hypothalamus (Critchley, 2005). The ratio of high-to-low frequency power in the cardiac spectrum is especially valuable. This ratio is assessed by using a Fourier analysis to evaluate several peaks in the frequency distribution of the beat-to-beat differences in resting heart rate when respiration is controlled. A higher frequency peak, at about 0.2 Hz, represents vagal influence. The lower frequency peak, 0.5–0.15 Hz, reflects both sympathetic and parasympathetic influences on heart rate due primarily to slower oscillations in blood pressure and body temperature, and the briskness of the baroreceptor reflex in the carotid sinus, which is controlled by changes in blood pressure (Loewy, 1990). High-reactive adolescents had greater cardiovascular sympathetic tone than low reactives.

These results are in accord with other reports (Davidson, 2003; Fox et al., 2005; Schmidt, Fox, Schulkin, & Gold, 1999). Among adults with a fear of flying, those who had low heart rate variability (reflecting greater sympathetic tone) reported more anxiety to pictures of airplanes than those who had greater heart rate variability (Bornas et al., 2005). Panic disorder patients had a larger than expected increase in blood pressure when they changed their posture from sitting to standing (Coupland et al., 2003). Finally, in a group of 52 adult males who experienced premature ejaculation (a sympathetically mediated reaction) a large proportion had shown symptoms of social anxiety preceding the sexual dysfunction (Corretti et al., 2006).

III. THE CURRENT STUDY

The interval between 11 and 14–17 years is marked by both biological maturation and diverse experiences. We wished to assess the degree to which the behavioral and physiological characteristics of the two temperamental types were preserved over the 4 years since our last assessment. This monograph summarizes the results of an assessment of a subset of the larger sample who were between 14 and 17 years of age; the mean and modal age was 15 years.

RATIONALE

Psychological Variables

The selection of behavioral variables was based on the assumption that high and low reactives would differ in talking, smiling, and motor tension while interacting with an unfamiliar examiner in a laboratory or during a home interview. Spontaneous talking, compared with restraint on speech, is mediated, in part, by projections from the amygdala to motor sites that mediate speech. Hence, we expected individuals with a more excitable amygdala to show an inhibition of spontaneous comments in unfamiliar social situations (Schulz et al., 2005). We further expected the two temperamental groups to vary in the focus of their primary worries, with high reactives more concerned with unfamiliar events they were unable to control. Accordingly, the interviewer asked questions about sources of anxiety. Adolescents also provided subjective perceptions of their personality characteristics, which were examined in connection with objective measures. Each participant was administered two *Q*-sort procedures. Finally, adolescents described their usual somatic reactions to a number of familiar situations.

In addition, the interviewer asked about the adolescents' religiosity. The conditions that contribute to a commitment to a formal religion are multiple and the balance among them varies with the historical era, culture, and age of the person, as well as the beliefs of their family. Thus, there is no single answer to the question of what determines a religious commitment that is valid across time or societies. It is possible, however, to discover some contributing conditions in current contexts. Youth in contemporary America are trying to establish their personal philosophy at a time when there is no consensus on the meaning of life or its origin. Further, the political commitment to egalitarianism has made individual achievement an urgently felt imperative. This combination of factors is uncommon in history and creates high levels of uncertainty in some adolescents. As a result, youths with a temperamental bias that renders them vulnerable to tension or worry might be motivated to find activities or belief systems that would mute their private angst. A religious commitment is one effective strategy because it provides a partial answer to the meaning of daily responsibilities and assures each believer of their essential value when disappointments, failures, or frustrations occur (Fischer et al., 2006; Hendricks-Ferguson, 2006; Masten et al., 2004).

Biological Variables

The selection of biological measures was guided by the same rationale that motivated the 11-year assessment. We assessed asymmetry of activation in the EEG, the ratio of β over α power in the EEG as an index of cortical arousal, the magnitude and latency of Wave 5 from the inferior colliculus, event-related potential waveforms to discrepant visual and semantic information, several measures of cardiovascular functioning (resting heart rates, spectral analysis of heart rate and blood pressure) and, finally, on a smaller sample, the ratio of the length of the index over the ring finger (the 2D:4D ratio). The reason for the latter variable is that several investigators have reported associations between the 2D:4D ratio and aspects of personality related to our temperamental categories. These data were available for only half the sample because they were gathered for a different purpose by a graduate student. Most males have a smaller ratio than females (i.e., the index finger is slightly shorter than the ring finger) because of the effect of prenatal androgen on the growth of the distal carpal on the ring finger of the fetus (Sanders et al., 2005; Roney & Maestripieri, 2004). Female fetuses lying next to their twin brother had smaller, more masculine, ratios than same sex female twins (van Anders, Vernon, & Wilbur, 2006).

High-reactive children, especially girls, have consistently smiled less often than low reactives, and we speculated that this difference might have biological correlates related to sex hormones. The human smile can accompany three quite different psychological states: (1) when individuals comprehend an initially difficult idea or achieve a goal following effort, (2) when they experience sensory pleasure, and (3) when they wish to signal a non-threatening posture or a desire to affiliate (Fridlund, 1994). The human smile is believed to be a phylogenetic derivative of the bared teeth grin of the chimpanzee, which is displayed when an animal is about to initiate an affiliative response (Parr, Walder, & Fogate, 2005; Waller & Dunbar, 2005). Females are less disposed than males to express physical aggression or to present a threatening posture (Hyde, 2005). The girls from all three temperamental groups smiled more often than boys at both 11 and 15 years. ($F_{(1, 229)} = 23.27$, $p < .001$ at age 11 in the laboratory; $F_{(1, 144)} = 27.5$, $p < .001$ at age 15 during the interview; $F_{(1, 68)} = 19.7$, $p < .001$ at age 15 in the laboratory). Thus, we were curious about the 2D:4D ratio in these adolescents.

METHOD

Participants

Laboratory assessments were conducted on 72 members of our longitudinal sample when they were between 14 and 17 years of age (mean age 15 years). These 72 adolescents were the oldest members of the longitudinal sample, but they did not differ from the remaining participants on demographic features or behaviors during preceding assessments. Forty of these 72 adolescents had been low reactive (20 girls) and 32 had been high reactive (13 girls). Only high and low reactives were evaluated in the laboratory. Only 72 adolescents were assessed in the laboratory because of the loss of facilities following the senior author's retirement.

These 72 adolescents were members of a larger group of 146 adolescents from this longitudinal sample that included 74 youths who were not seen in the laboratory. This larger group was comprised of 59 low reactives (30 girls), 49 high reactives (26 girls), and 38 from the other temperamental group (24 girls) (low motor combined with high crying or high motor combined with low crying). These 146 participants were visited at home, where they responded to a lengthy interview, two Q-sorts, and a series of questions inquiring about their usual somatic reactions to different situations. The 74 adolescents who were interviewed, but not seen in the laboratory, were the next oldest members of the sample. They did not differ in demographic features or prior behaviors from the participants who were not seen for this assessment.

During the interview nine adolescents—all girls—reported that they had been diagnosed by a psychiatrist as depressed and were under psychiatric care; five had been high reactive, one low reactive and three were from the other temperamental group. One high-reactive boy was diagnosed with anxiety disorder, and one boy from the other temperamental group had been diagnosed with ADHD. Thus, 11 of the 146 adolescents belonged to a DSM psychiatric category according to their report. We did not conduct a psychiatric interview with them. However, all 11 were in school and dealing moderately well with their daily responsibilities.

We have been critical of the assumption that inferences based on self-reports are valid substitutes for direct behavioral observations (Kagan & Snidman, 2004). Buttressing our position, a meta-analysis of 27 studies with questionnaire data on extraversion, neuroticism, and emotional expressiveness, as well as observations of emotional expressiveness, revealed that the two sources of evidence had different meanings and the self-reports should not be treated as equivalent to the observed behaviors (Riggio & Riggio, 2002). This position does not mean, however, that self-reports of emotions or personality features lack psychological value. Although we do not assume that all adolescents who say they worry about school failure or report being unhappy, compared with those who deny these features, would necessarily display behavioral or biological signs supporting their verbal statements. But these statements likely have theoretical significance because individuals' descriptions of their feelings and traits are influenced, in part, by their ego ideal. Adults who deny feeling angry or anxious may show signs of these states in their behavior and biology, and their denial could reflect a significant personal characteristic.

PROCEDURES

Laboratory Evaluation

Behavior

A coder, blind to the adolescent's past history or temperamental classification, coded a filmed record for the number of spontaneous comments and smiles displayed during the initial 40 minutes of the laboratory session while the examiner gathered heart rate, blood pressure, and administered a test for auditory acuity but before the placement of electrodes for the EEG and ERP recordings and the instruction to remain quiet. These behavioral variables had separated high and low reactives at every prior assessment (Kagan & Snidman, 2004).

Biological Variables

For the EEG, ERP and Wave 5 procedures electrodes were placed according to the international 10/20 system at F3, Fz, F4, P3, Pz, P4, M1, M2, and referenced to Cz. Vertical eye movements were recorded from electrodes placed super- and suborbitally on the left eye, and horizontal eye movements were recorded from the same electrodes placed at the outer canthus of each eye. Data were sampled at 1,000 Hz, and signals were band-pass filtered between .08 and 100 Hz. The data were resampled at 512 Hz and re-referenced to average linked mastoids offline. The waveforms were inspected visually for eye movement or muscle artifacts. When an artifact was identified on any channel, all data on all channels were excluded for that time interval.

EEG

The subject sat quietly with eyes open for 2 minutes. α power was defined as the sum of spectral power between 8 and 13 Hz; β power as the sum of spectral power between 14 and 30 Hz. The spectral power estimates were log-transformed to normalize the distribution. Asymmetry of activation was computed by subtracting log α power on the left from log α power on the right; hence, a positive value reflected less α power and therefore greater activation on the left side. Data were available for 61 adolescents.

Event-Related Potential: N100 and N400 to Pictures

A set of chromatic pictures was displayed in a darkened room on a TV monitor placed one meter in front of the subject. Each picture was shown for 1,000 ms with an inter-stimulus interval of 1,200 ms. Data were collected for a 50 ms prestimulus baseline and for the duration of the picture. An observer noted if the subject failed to pay attention to any picture. Data were available for 66 adolescents. Blocks of ecologically valid pictures alternated with blocks of ecologically invalid pictures with 20 pictures in each block. Blocks 1, 3, and 5 displayed the valid pictures and blocks 2, 4, and 6 the invalid pictures. All 120 pictures were unique, and none was suggestive of disgust, fear, anger, or sadness.

The individual ERP waveforms to each picture were combined to produce average waveforms for the valid and invalid categories of pictures. The mean integrated voltage for each picture category had to contain a minimum of 12 values from each block of 20 pictures. A visual inspection of the grand averages, using all leads and both picture types, identified two components. One variable was the total amount of negative voltage integrated from 100 to 180 ms; the second area was the integrated voltage from 350 to 450 ms. These two variables were computed separately for each class of picture at frontal, central, and parietal sites. In an oddball paradigm adults showed larger N100 waveforms to infrequent, compared with frequent, stimuli (Potts, Patel, & Azzam, 2004); and very brief exposures of masked faces with a fearful expression that are not detected consciously evoke more activity in the brainstem and amygdala than faces with neutral expressions (Liddell et al., 2005; Carlsson et al., 2004). These facts suggest that the brain detects some features of salient stimuli within the first 100–150 ms. Therefore, the adolescents in our sample should have been able to respond differentially to the valid and invalid scenes within the first 150 ms.

ERP (N400) to Semantic Incongruity

A series of 80 short sentences (four to six words in length) composed of familiar words were constructed. One-half of the sentences were semantically congruent; the other half had a final word that rendered the sentence semantically incongruent. (These words were supplied by Philip Holcomb of Tufts University.) Each word appeared on the TV monitor for 300 ms with an interstimulus interval of 500 ms between each word, and 1,300 ms between the last word of a sentence and the first word of the next sentence. A fixation cross appeared for 300 ms at a point 800 ms before the first word of each new sentence. The variable of interest was the ERP waveform following the last word in each of the 80 sentences. These waveforms were combined to produce average waveforms for the two categories of sentences, valid and invalid, and the integrated voltage from 350 to 450 ms was computed for the N400. A total of 53 adolescents had valid data on this episode (25 high reactives and 28 low reactives). Seventeen participants were excluded because they blinked whenever a word appeared on the screen, and this reaction seriously contaminated the resulting waveform.

Heart Rate

Heart rate electrodes were placed in a standard configuration on the subject's chest. Baseline heart rate was collected while the subject sat quietly for 2 minutes and also while the subject was in a standing posture. The subject was then asked to lay supine on a comfortable mat and breathe in time to a computer-generated waveform which cycled at .25 Hz for 3 minutes. The data were analyzed using a fast Fourier transformation (FFT) to characterize the frequency distribution of the cardiac signal. The variable of interest was the ratio of high ($>.2$ Hz) to low (.5–1.5 Hz) frequency power in the cardiac spectrum that represents the ratio of vagal to sympathetic and parasympathetic influences. Data were available for 57 adolescents. We also assessed systolic and diastolic blood pressure in sitting and standing postures and data were available for 69 participants.

Wave 5

Each child was screened for ear health prior to measuring the BAER. The screening included a medical history from the parent and a test of auditory acuity (a two-alternative procedure at 2,000 Hz). Earphones were first placed on the subject's head. The adolescent was told that two lights placed one meter in front would be lit in succession, but a tone would only be transmitted through the earphones when one of the lights was lit; when the other light came on there would be no tone. After both lights had lit, the adolescent indicated which light was associated with the presentation of the tone. Four tones that became increasingly softer were presented. The few children with impaired hearing were excluded from the analysis.

Following the acuity test, data were collected at Cz, M1, and M2. The adolescent heard through an earphone on the right ear a series of 2,200 clicks of alternating polarity (0.1 ms clicks; 70 dBspl presented at a rate of 27 per second. The recording epoch was 37 ms (10 ms were utilized for analysis). Waveforms were band-pass filtered at .08 to 3,000 Hz. The data were digitized at 10,000 Hz and digitially refiltered at 30–30,000 Hz. The peaks and troughs of Waves 3 and 5 from the reference electrode, contralateral to the stimulated ear, were identified with a computer algorithm and checked manually by a coder unaware of the child's temperamental category. The contralateral values are more sensitive than the ipsilateral values because more fibers cross from the basilar membrane on the right side to the left hemisphere. The variables of interest were the difference (in microvolts) between the trough of Wave 3 and the peak of Wave 5, and the latency to the peak of Wave 5. Data were available for 60 adolescents.

Home Interview

The home interviews were conducted by one of two women. Neither woman had any knowledge of the adolescent's temperamental category at 4 months or their past history. The filmed interviews, which lasted from 90 to 120 minutes, dealt with the adolescent's academic interests and performance, extracurricular activities, sources of worry, sadness, anger, empathy, joy, and guilt, as well as attitudes toward religion and society.

A coder, also without knowledge of the adolescent's past history or infant temperament, studied each filmed interview and rated four behavioral variables (each on a 4-point scale) based on behavior during the entire interview. The four behavioral variables rated were: amount of talking, frequency of smiling, degree of postural tension together with frequency of hand and limb movements, and, finally, an overall rating of behavioral inhibition based primarily on the absence of talking and smiling, but including excessive motoricity, defensiveness, a soft voice, and frequent turning away from the examiner. A rating of 1 for each of the four variables reflected an uninhibited persona; a rating of 4 reflected an inhibited style. Thus, an adolescent who received a 1 for behavioral inhibition talked and smiled frequently, showed minimal motor tension, and no defensiveness; whereas an adolescent who received a rating of 4 gave minimally elaborated replies, rarely smiled, showed frequent motor tension, a soft voice, and an extreme level of defensiveness.

The coder also rated each adolescent's degree of religiosity based on answers to five questions about their religious beliefs. The adolescents were asked whether they thought a spiritual or metaphysical force made any contribution to life, whether and how regularly they attended religious services, whether attendance at religious services made them feel good, whether they prayed regularly, and whether they had any experience that persuaded them that God might exist. Each adolescent was classified as religious if they attended religious services regularly, derived a feeling of satisfaction from this experience, prayed often, and awarded some power for life on earth to a spiritual force (even if they accepted the validity of scientific positions on the origins of the universe and life).

A second, independent coder, also blind to the adolescent's history, rated these five variables on 35 randomly selected participants. Kappa values for talking, smiling, motoricity, overall inhibition, and religiosity were high, ranging from .76 to .81.

Q-sorts

Each adolescent completed two Q-sorts—one during and one at the end of the interview. The first Q-sort consisted of 15 statements dealing with sources of worry; the second consisted of 20 statements describing personality traits. Table 1 lists the items from the two Q-sorts. Each adolescent ranked each statement with respect to how accurately it characterized the self. (Five of the 146 adolescents did not fill out Q-sorts because of time constraints.)

Somatic Reactions

Each adolescent indicated which of six somatic reactions occurred to each of nine situations. The nine situations, which were read to the adolescent by the interviewer, were: meeting a stranger, speaking in front of the class, criticism from a teacher, criticism from a parent, insects, storms, being alone at home, being snubbed by a peer, and exposure to a large quantity of blood. The somatic reactions, which were printed on cards, and placed in front of the adolescent, were: sweating of the palms, a rise in heart rate, difficulty breathing, flushing of the face, muscle tension, and stomach tension. (Nine of the 146 adolescents did not complete this procedure.)

This procedure derives from evidence regarding physiological components of awareness of bodily states. Afferent feedback from the cardiovascular system, gut, skin, respiratory, and skeletal muscles, carried by sympathetic or parasympathetic fibers, synapses in the medulla and is integrated in the parabrachial nucleus within the pons region of the

TABLE 1

Q-SORT PROCEDURES

Q-Sort 1: Worries
1. Having enough money when I am an adult.
2. Being alone.
3. Having enough time to finish my school work.
4. Not doing well in school.
5. Not doing well in extracurricular activities (band/orchestra, sports, theater).
6. How smart I am.
7. How I dress.
8. A terrorist attack.
9. My parents being disappointed in me.
10. My future.
11. Not having friends.
12. Dirt on something clean I am wearing.
13. Being pressured by my friends to do something I don't want to do.
14. Being popular.
15. How physically attractive I am.

Q-Sort 2: Personality
1. I feel bad if my father or mother criticizes me.
2. I often wonder what my friends think of me.
3. I worry about getting a bad grade.
4. I don't like disagreeing with my friends.
5. Most of the time I am happy.
6. I like going to new places I haven't seen.
7. I prefer being with a lot of my friends rather than one or two.
8. I laugh easily.
9. I am pretty serious.
10. I am shy with adults I don't know.
11. I am shy with other kids I don't know.
12. I like doing things that are a little risky.
13. I like exciting experiences like roller coasters.
14. I make new friends easily.
15. I make decisions too quickly.
16. I think too much before deciding what to do.
17. I like doing things that make my friends laugh.
18. I think of myself as easy-going.
19. I wish I were more relaxed.
20. I startle easily to loud sounds.

brainstem. This information is sent to the postro-medial nucleus of the thalamus and then to the amygdala, insula, anterior cingulate, and orbito-frontal prefrontal cortex. It has been suggested that activity in the right anterior insula provides a critical foundation for the consciousness of one's bodily state, compared with an awareness of external events (Craig, 2003).

Analytic Plan

The analyses of this large corpus of data were guided by several a priori ideas. First, as always, we examined the differences among the temperamental and gender groups for each variable with ANOVA before imposing other analyses. Second, we occasionally examined extreme scores, rather than relying only on mean values. We justify this practice on the grounds that it is usually the case that, when a significant correlation between two variables is less than .5, the relation is rarely linear and is due to individuals with values in the top or bottom 20–25% of the distribution.

The nine behavioral variables examined were the following: talking and smiling during the interview and the laboratory, interview ratings of inhibition, motoricity, and religiosity, a Q-sort variable reflecting a sanguine or a dour personality based on four items from the Q-sort, and the mean number of somatic reactions reported for four evaluative situations. The 17 biological variables quantified were asymmetry of frontal α power in the EEG, the ratio of β–α power at rest in frontal sites, the magnitude and latency of Wave 5 to the hemisphere contralateral to the ear receiving the stimuli, the difference in integrated voltages of the event-related potential to invalid versus valid scenes for each successive pair of blocks for both the N400 and the N100 waveforms, the difference in integrated voltage between the invalid and valid sentences, the spectral analysis of heart rate, and resting heart rate in a sitting position, systolic and diastolic blood pressure under sitting and standing postures. Table 2 lists the means and standard deviations for all the variables and Table 3 lists the results of the ANOVAs that yielded significant effects for temperament, gender, or the temperament by gender interaction.

TABLE 2
MEANS AND STANDARD DEVIATIONS FOR VARIABLES WITH SIGNIFICANT EFFECTS FOR TEMPERAMENT, SEX, OR INTERACTION

	Low-Reactive		High-Reactive		Other	
	Boys	Girls	Boys	Girls	Boys	Girls
Laboratory						
Smile	10.9 (9.0)	27.5 (21.9)	5.5 (5.7)	17.4 (9.1)		
Talk	21.4 (12.9)	25.6 (16.5)	15.9 (12.5)	21.9 (12.7)		
BP Diastolic Sit	59.4 (7.6)	61.8 (7.7)	59.1 (6.3)	65.5 (5.9)		
BP Diastolic Stand	63.1 (6.6)	64.7 (7.7)	62.4 (7.7)	66.9 (6.5)		
BP Systolic Sit	131.7 (9.0)	121.5 (11.2)	128.5 (9.6)	125.9 (6.8)		
BP Systolic Stand	130.7 (9.4)	121.7 (11.4)	128.1 (10.8)	127.3 (9.3)		
EEG β/α	.92 (.2)	1.01 (.2)	.95 (.2)	.94 (.2)		
EEG Frontal Asymmetry	.03 (.1)	.09 (.1)	.01 (.1)	.01 (.1)		
ERP N100 Pictures I–V Blocks 1+2	−.80 (5.1)	−1.45 (6.3)	1.53 (4.6)	−.59 (6.1)		
ERP N100 Pictures I–V Blocks 3+4	.01 (5.2)	1.44 (2.9)	.54 (5.04)	.71 (5.1)		
ERP N100 Pictures I–V Blocks 5+6	1.62 (5.8)	−2.16 (7.5)	−4.90 (9.6)	−1.77 (3.4)		
ERP N400 Pictures I–V Blocks 1+2	.04 (5.8)	−3.26 (7.3)	−1.6 (7.4)	.84 (5.1)		
ERP N400 Pictures I–V Blocks 3+4	−4.71 (3.3)	−1.65 (4.6)	−.88 (8.2)	−1.29 (4.1)		
ERP N400 Pictures I–V Blocks 5+6	−1.12 (5.8)	−2.90 (7.6)	−2.28 (8.0)	−3.89 (4.8)		
ERP N400 Sentences Mean I–V	−1.2 (4.2)	−.1 (3.9)	−2.2 (4.1)	.2 (4.4)		
Heart Rate Baseline	973.2 (105.3)	838.9 (103.3)	918.4 (107.6)	844.9 (79.2)		
Parasympathetic/Sympathetic	1.8 (1.9)	1.1 (1.2)	1.4 (1.7)	1.0 (1.0)		
Wave V Contra Amplitude	.52 (.13)	.52 (.15)	.56 (.20)	.54 (.22)		
Wave V Contra Latency	5.5 (.20)	5.4 (.13)	5.4 (.21)	5.2 (.26)		
Interview						
Inhibition	1.6 (.6)	1.8 (.8)	2.6 (.7)	1.9 (.8)	1.7 (.8)	1.5 (.6)
Motoricity	1.6 (.7)	1.8 (.8)	2.6 (.7)	2.0 (.7)	1.6 (.8)	1.6 (.7)
Sanguine	13.9 (3.4)	12.9 (3.1)	12.8 (3.2)	11.7 (3.6)	10.6 (2.4)	11.4 (2.0)
Smile	2.4 (.8)	1.5 (.7)	2.9 (1.0)	2.1 (.7)	2.2 (.9)	1.7 (.8)
Somatic Reaction	1.5 (.7)	1.7 (.8)	1.5 (.6)	1.6 (.8)	1.6 (.8)	1.6 (.7)
Talk	1.8 (.9)	1.3 (.5)	2.2 (1.1)	1.4 (.8)	1.6 (.8)	1.4 (.5)

TABLE 3
Significant Effects for Temperament, Sex or Interaction

	Temperament			Sex			Interaction			Variance
Variable	df	F	p	df	F	p	df	F	p	R^2
Laboratory										
Smiles	1, 67	5.86	.01	1, 67	19.74	<.001	NS			.29
Latency Wave 5	1, 58	7.2	<.01	1, 58	7.67	<.01	NS			.19
Interview										
Talk	NS			1, 140	12.3	<.001	NS			
Smiles	2, 140	6.90	<.01	1, 140	26.3	<.001	NS			.24
Motoricity	2, 140	10.9	<.001	NS			2, 140	4.0	<.05	.17
Inhibition	2, 140	16.5	<.001	1, 140	8.7	<.01	NS			.25
Sanguine	2, 135	6.3	<.01	NS			NS			.11

IV. RESULTS

LABORATORY BEHAVIOR

Although there was no difference between the low or high reactives in the number of spontaneous comments during the first 40 minutes of the laboratory session, high reactives smiled significantly less often than low reactives ($F_{(1,68)} = 5.86$, $p = .01$), and girls smiled more than boys ($F_{(1,68)} = 19.74$, $p < .001$). There was no interaction between temperament and gender. High reactives have consistently displayed fewer spontaneous smiles than low reactives when interacting with a stranger in an unfamiliar situation.

INTERVIEW BEHAVIOR

Motoricity

The rating of motoricity (based on hand and leg movements and postural tension) clearly separated the high and low reactives ($F_{(2,140)} = 10.89$, $p < .001$), with no effect of gender, but there was a gender by temperament interaction because high-reactive males had very high ratings of motoricity. Forty-nine percent of high reactives, but only 16% of low reactives and others, received a rating of 3 or 4 for motor tension ($\chi^2(1) = 21.6$, $p < .001$). High reactives had shown significantly more tension in the corrugator muscle of the forehead while watching unpleasant, pleasant, and neutral pictures during the laboratory evaluation of potentiated startle at 11 years of age (Kagan & Snidman, 2004).

Talking and Smiling

A majority of girls from all three temperamental groups talked and smiled frequently during the interview and, as a result, high- and low-reactive girls did not differ significantly on these variables. However, high-reactive boys talked less often and were rated as more inhibited than low-reactive boys ($t(50) = 1.92$, $p = .05$ for talking; $t(50) = 4.98$, $p < .001$ for rating of inhibition).

TABLE 4

PERCENT OF LOW-REACTIVE, HIGH-REACTIVE, AND OTHER BOYS GIVEN RATINGS OF 3 OR 4
(SUBDUED) FOR TALKING, SMILING, AND BEHAVIORAL INHIBITION DURING THE INTERVIEW

Variable	Low Reactive (%)	Other (%)	High Reactive (%)
Talking	24	7	43
Smiling	38	29	61
Inhibition	10	21	61

Table 4 contains the percentage of high-reactive, low-reactive, and other boys who received a rating of 3 or 4 (inhibited persona) for talking, smiling, and overall inhibition. By contrast, 55% of low-reactive boys, but only one high-reactive boy, received a rating of 1 on inhibition, whereas 61% of high-reactive boys, compared with only 10% of low-reactive boys, received a rating of 3 or 4 ($\chi^2(1) = 15.2, p < .001$). Three of the four adolescents who did not look at the interviewer for most of the 2-hour session—a very unusual reaction—had been high-reactive boys.

Twenty-seven of the 49 high reactives interviewed at age 15 had been observed at $4\frac{1}{2}$ years of age in a peer play situation consisting of three children of the same sex and age, who were unfamiliar with each other, playing in a laboratory setting with all three parents present (Kagan, Snidman, & Arcus, 1998). Thirteen of the 27 high reactives had been classified as extremely inhibited in this play situation, whereas the remaining 14 were less inhibited (very few low reactives were inhibited in this setting). Seven of the 13 inhibited 4-year-olds were rated as inhibited during the interview at age 15 (rating of 3 or 4), compared with only three of the 14 who were not inhibited during the play session ($p < .05$ by the Exact Test).

Relation to Fear in the Second Year

Seventy-one percent of the 15-year-old low reactives, but only 26% of high reactives and 43% of others, had displayed very low fear scores to unfamiliar events in the second year (mean fear score at 14 and 21 months was ≤ 2.0; $\chi^2(2) = 21.8, p < .001$). However, level of fearful behavior in the second year, when considered alone and ignoring 4-month temperament, did not predict behavior in the laboratory or during the home interview. The 4-month temperamental category was not a less sensitive predictor of interview behavior than the combination of 4-month temperament and fear score in the second year. This fact implies that the tendency to approach or to avoid unfamiliar people or objects in the second year of life can be a learned reaction. Several low reactives who were uninhibited at ages 11 and 15 had high fear scores at 21 months.

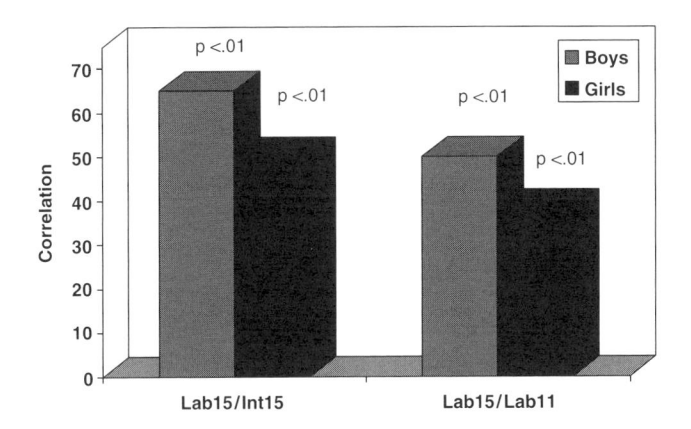

FIGURE 1.—Correlations for smiling between laboratory and home.

Smiling in Laboratory and Home

Figure 1 illustrates the correlations between frequency of smiling in the laboratory and during the home interview, and the relation between smiling in the laboratory at 11 and 15 years (sexes separately). The adolescents were relatively consistent in their tendency to smile in the laboratory and at home ($r = .58$, $p < .01$ across all subjects), and there was modest intra-individual stability of smiling in the laboratory from 11 to 15 years of age ($r = .47$, $p < .001$).

We assigned the high and low reactives to one of two groups, based on frequency of smiling in the laboratory and at home. The high smiling group, who received a rating of 1 for smiling during the interview and had a value for laboratory smiles equal to or above the median, consisted of 14 low reactives and four high reactives. The low smiling group, who received a rating of 3 or 4 for smiling during the interview and had a value for laboratory smiles below the median, contained seven low reactives and 11 high reactives ($\chi^2(1) = 7.4$, $p < .01$).

Relation of Smiles to 2D:4D Ratio

The 2D:4D data affirmed the usual sex difference in the ratio. More important, the low-reactive girls, who smiled more than any other group at every evaluation, with ratios $\geq .99$ smiled more frequently at both 11 and 15 years of age than low-reactive girls with smaller, more masculine ratios ($p < .05$ by the Exact Test). Further, adolescents with ratios in the top quartile of the distribution (mean ratio for the two hands $\geq .99$) smiled more frequently than others during the laboratory session at 14 months ($\chi^2(1) = 7.2$, $p < .01$). The two boys with the largest ratios (> 1.0) were high reactives who, during the interview, said they were easily intimidated and tried to avoid confrontations with others.

Sources of Worry

Three questions posed at different times during the interview asked each adolescent to report the targets of their worries. The questions were: "What things make you nervous or anxious?" "What do you worry about?" "Can you name two times you were worried over the past few months?" The answers fell into one of five categories that resembled the factors derived from a fear survey of over 800 adults (Fisher et al., 2006). The categories of worry were: (1) quality of performance in school or extracurricular activities; (2) uncertainty over encounters with unfamiliar people, places, or situations, or the inability to know the future; (3) social rejection and maintaining friendships; (4) physical harm; and (5) worries over the health of a relative or pet.

Worry over competent performance in school or extracurricular activities was named most frequently (54% cited only this concern). Low reactives were more likely than high reactives or others to nominate performance as their only source of worry to all three questions (61% of low reactives vs. 37% of high reactives and 55% of others). By contrast, 67% of high reactives named encounters with crowds, unfamiliar peers, visits to new places, or the inability to know the future as a serious source of worry to at least one of the questions, compared with 20% of low reactives and 29% of others ($\chi^2(2) = 19.0, p < .001$). Every one of the 11 high-reactive adolescents (five boys and six girls) who became so distressed during the final episode of the 4-month assessment the session had to be terminated named unfamiliarity as a source of worry during the interview.

Some verbatim excerpts illustrate the concern with unfamiliar or unpredictable situations among high reactives: "In a crowd I feel isolated and left out, I don't know what to pay attention to because it is all so ambiguous"; "I worry about the future, over not knowing what will happen next"; "I wanted to be a doctor but decided against it because I felt it would be too much of a strain"; "I like being alone and, therefore, horses are my hobby, I don't have to worry about fitting in with others when I am with my horses"; "I get nervous before every vacation because I don't know what will happen." Similar statements were rare among low reactives or others.

Religiosity

Thirty-three percent of the participants in the sample were classified as religious and the remaining two-thirds as nonreligious, a value close to the estimate of 42% of Americans who regularly attend religious services (Wuthnow, 2006). The distributions of family religions were similar for the three temperamental groups; 40% of the families were Catholic, 30% Protestant, 25% Jewish, 4% belonged to another religion, and 1% denied any religious affiliation. Forty-five percent of the youths who had been high reactive were classified as religious, compared with 25% of low reactives and 28% of the others ($\chi^2(2) = 4.4$, $p < .05$). Although the religious adolescents were more likely to have grown up in religious homes (85% had one or both parents who attended religious services regularly), there was no significant difference between high and low reactives in parental religious commitment.

Further, the ratio of power in the β over the α band, gathered while each adolescent sat quietly with eyes open, was higher for the nonreligious than the religious adolescents ($F_{(1, 57)} = 3.85$, $p < .05$), with no interaction with temperament or gender. Because the higher β–α ratio reflects a higher level of cortical arousal, this result implies that religious youth may have been less apprehensive in the laboratory situation. Not one of the five clinically depressed high-reactive girls was religious; not one of the religious high-reactive girls was under psychiatric care.

Q-Sorts

We created an index of a sanguine compared with a dour mood by averaging the ranks for four highly correlated Q-sort items (see Table 1, numbers 9, 16, 18, and 19): "I am pretty serious," "I think too much before deciding what to do," "I wish I were more relaxed," and the reverse of "I'm easy-going." High scores reflect a sanguine mood; low scores a dour mood. Low reactives were more likely than high reactives or others to describe themselves as sanguine ($F_{(2, 135)} = 6.34$, $p < .01$), with no significant effect of gender and no interaction. This difference was only significant for the comparison of low reactives with others. Forty-one percent of low reactives, compared with 23% of high reactives and none of the other temperamental group, had a mean rank equal to greater than the average value of 15 for this variable ($\chi^2(2) = 19.2$, $p < .001$).

High and low reactives also differed significantly in the rank assigned to the single item from the Q-sort: "Most of the time I'm happy." High reactives described themselves as less happy than the two other groups ($F_{(2, 138)} = 12.66$, $p < .001$), and there was no interaction with gender. The statement, "I'm happy most of the time" was the only item also present in the Q-sort administered to this sample when they were 11 years old. More low than high reactives or others reported being happy at both ages ($\chi^2(2) = 13.8$, $p < .01$). A repeated measures analysis of variance revealed a significant effect of temperament ($F_{(2, 122)} = 6.16$, $p < .01$) and

TABLE 5

PERCENT OF THE "HAPPY" ADOLESCENTS (RANKS 1–4) RANKING OTHER ITEMS AS CHARACTERISTIC OF SELF

Item	Low Reactive (%)	High Reactive (%)
I laugh easily (ranks 1–3)	46	25
I'm easy-going (ranks 1–3)	32	16
I'm too serious (ranks 1–8)	8	25
I think too much (ranks 1–8)	13	33

gender ($F_{(1, 122)} = 3.69$, $p < .05$), with boys happier than girls, but no interaction between temperament and gender. The low-reactive boys were distinctive. Fifty-four percent reported being happier at age 15 than at age 11 (rank at 15 was lower than the rank at 11), whereas high-reactive girls were least likely to be happier at the older age (only 16% of high-reactive girls did so).

However, the personal meaning of the endorsement "Most of the time I'm happy" varied with the youth's temperament because high and low reactives endorsing this item (they placed it in the first four ranks) gave different ranks to four other Q-sort items related to mood. Two items reflected a serious mood ("I'm too serious" and "I think too much"); two items reflected a relaxed mood ("I laugh easily" and "I'm easy-going"). More low than high reactives who said they were "happy" ranked the two relaxed items as characteristic of self (46 and 32%), whereas the "happy" high reactives ranked the two items reflecting a serious mood as more characteristic of self (25% and 33%) (see Table 5; $\chi^2 = 8.5$, $p < .01$). Thus, high and low reactives possessed different understandings of, or semantic connotations to, the word "happy" as applied to self.

Maternal Q-Sorts of 11-Year-Olds

The mothers of 90% of this sample had ranked 28 statements describing their child at 11 years in a Q-sort procedure (Kagan & Snidman, 2004). We asked whether these maternal descriptions predicted the adolescent's interview behavior or Q-sorts at age 15. Four correlated items in the maternal Q-sort described a shy, inhibited child (shy with other children he or she doesn't know, shy with unfamiliar adults, worries about what might happen in the future, and becomes quiet and subdued in unfamiliar places). Five correlated items described an uninhibited personality (has a lot of friends, is easy-going, talks a lot with other children, likes to try new things, and is outgoing with other boys and girls). The mean of each set was computed and, as expected, the correlation between the two means was negative

($r = -.61$). We subtracted one mean from the other so that a positive score reflected a maternal description of an inhibited child.

There was only a modest relation between the maternal descriptions at age 11 and the rating of adolescent inhibition in the interview at age 15 ($r = .29$ for boys and .30 for girls, $p < .05$), and no predictive relation to the adolescents' Q-sorts. The maternal descriptions were only accurate for three high reactives (6% of that group) who were extremely inhibited during the interview (they received a rating of 4). Only 7 of 24 children described by their parent as inhibited at age 11 showed inhibited behavior during the interview; whereas 18 of 21 children described as inhibited had been high reactive. Thus, the 4 month infant temperamental category was a better predictor of behavior during the interview than the mother's descriptions of these children when they were 11 years old.

Somatic Reactions

The participants were most likely to report somatic reactions to the four situations in which they were being evaluated by another (meeting a stranger, speaking in front of the class, and when a teacher or a parent criticized them). Each of these four evaluative situations was associated with a slightly different profile of somatic reactions. Because few adolescents reported breathing difficulties or stomach or muscle tension, we pooled these three reactions into one category. Speaking in front of the class was most often associated with reports of increased heart rate; teacher criticism with facial flushing; parental criticism with breathing or stomach or muscle tension; and meeting a stranger with sweating of the palms. Few reported somatic reactions to insects, storms, being alone at home, being snubbed by a peer, or seeing a large amount of blood. Young adults from different nations also reported fear of evaluation by others more frequently than fear of bodily harm, witnessing aggression, or small animals, such as insects and mice (Arrindell et al., 2003).

We computed the mean number of somatic reactions reported to the four evaluative situations (mean = 1.5, $SD = .7$, median 1.5 and range of .25–4.75). An ANOVA revealed no significant difference attributable to temperament, in part, because most adolescents reported somatic reactions to evaluation of their performances in and out of school. However, 15 of 20 adolescents combined frequent somatic reports (greater than the mean) with high systolic blood pressure values at age 11 ($z \geq .5$). Eleven of these 15 named unfamiliarity as a primary source of worry during the interview, and only 4 named performance. By contrast, only 6 of 22 adolescents who had infrequent somatic reports (less than the mean) and lower systolic blood pressure ($z < -.5$) named unfamiliarity as a primary source of worry while 11 named performance ($\chi^2(1) = 10.8$, $p < .01$; see Table 6).

TABLE 6

RELATION OF SYSTOLIC BLOOD PRESSURE AT AGE 11 AND SOMATIC REPORTS TO SOURCES OF WORRY

	Somatic Reports	
Systolic Blood Pressure	High	Low
High $z > .5$	$N = 20$ 10 HR 5 LR 5 0	$N = 19$ 9 HR 7 LR 3 0
Low $z < -.5$	$N = 16$ 2 HR 9 LR 5 0	$N = 22$ 6 HR 8 LR 8 0

BIOLOGY

EEG Asymmetry

The difference in the log of α power between left and right frontal sites (F3 and F4) revealed that 71% of low reactives but 52% of high reactives were left frontal active (difference $> .00$), a difference that missed the conventional level of significance ($\chi^2 = 2.7$). However, the display of left or right frontal activation was moderately stable from 11 to 15 years of age ($r = .43$, $p < .01$ for low reactives; $r = .34$, $p = .09$ for high reactives; $r = .40$, $p < .01$ for the entire sample). Furthermore, more high than low reactives showed greater activation on the right, compared with the left, frontal sites (less α power at F4 than at F3) at both 11 and 15 years of age (28% vs. 5%), whereas more low reactives were left frontal active at both ages (34% vs. 24%, $\chi^2 = 4.7$, $p < .05$). In contrast to the data at 11 years of age, there was no temperamental difference in asymmetry of activation at parietal sites.

A significant effect of temperament also emerged when both the rating of inhibition during the interview and frontal asymmetry were treated as dependent variables ($F_{(1,57)} = 15.79$, $p < .01$), with no effect for gender and no interaction. Low reactives were more likely than high reactives (69% vs. 24%) to combine uninhibited interview behavior (a rank of 1 or 2) with left frontal activation; only 16% of high-reactive girls displayed both features.

β–α Ratio

The ratio of β over α power in frontal sites with eyes open was stable from 11 to 15 years ($r = .60$, $p < .01$ for low reactives; $r = .51$, $p < .01$ for high reactives; $r = .56$, $p < .01$ for the entire sample), but this variable did not separate the temperamental groups. Although there was no relation between frontal asymmetry and the β–α ratio, high reactives were more likely

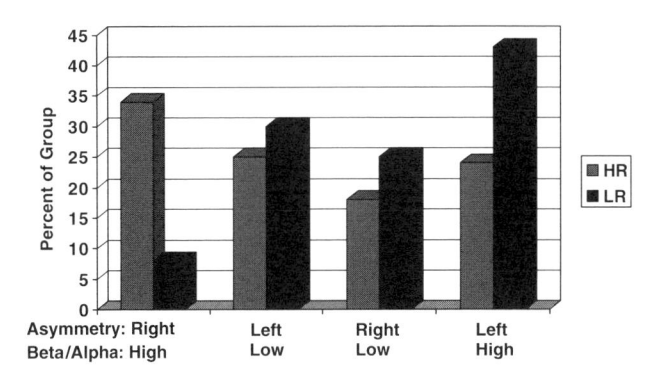

FIGURE 2.—Temperamental differences in β–α ratio and asymmetry of activation.

than low reactives to combine a high β–α ratio (above the median value of .90) with right frontal activation (32% vs. 10%), whereas low reactives were more likely to combine a high β–α ratio with left frontal activation (43% vs. 24%; $\chi^2(1) = 5.6$, $p < .05$; see Figure 2). Studies of adults suggest high heritability of α and β power values ($h^2 = .87$ for α and .86 for β at frontal sites) (Smit, Posthuma, Boomsma, & DeGeus, 2005), and for the functional connectivity of α and β frequency bands (Posthuma et al., 2005).

Wave 5

The two variables quantified from the brainstem auditory evoked potential were the magnitude of Wave 5 (the difference between the trough of Wave 3 and the peak of Wave 5) and the latency to the peak of Wave 5. Although the high reactives had slightly larger Wave 5 magnitudes than low reactives (.55 vs. .52 μV), the difference missed statistical significance. However, this variable, too, was stable from 11 to 15 years ($r = .64$, $p < .01$). As was true for EEG asymmetry, more high than low reactives had larger Wave 5 magnitudes (greater than the mean) at both 11 and 15 years (40% vs. 0%), whereas more low than high reactives had values below the mean at both ages (40 vs. 24%, $\chi^2(1) = 10.3$, $p < .001$).

Second, high reactives had a significantly faster latency to the peak of Wave 5 than low reactives ($F_{(1,58)} = 7.20$, $p = .01$), and more high than low reactives combined a latency faster than the mean with an amplitude greater than the mean (28% vs. 8%), whereas more low reactives showed the opposite profile (31% vs. 8%, $\chi^2(1) = 6.9$, $p < .05$). As at age 11, there was no relation between the magnitude of or latency to Wave 5 and behavior during the interview or the adolescents' Q-sort profiles. However, the only biological variable assessed at age 11 that separated the five high-reactive girls who reported during the interview that they were clinically depressed from the remaining 21 high-reactive girls was a large Wave 5 (four of the five depressed girls had values $>.80\,\mu V$, compared with 8 of the 21 non-depressed, high-reactive girls).

N400 to the Pictures

A repeated measures analysis of variance on the six blocks of pictures revealed a significant difference in integrated voltage among the six blocks ($F_{(5,318)} = 10.3, p < .001$), with significantly larger values to the invalid than to the valid pictures ($F_{(1,62)} = 18.8, p < .001$). Although the mean difference between invalid and valid pictures (I–V difference) was not associated with temperament, the high and low reactives differed with respect to the block pair during which they showed their largest I–V difference.

Seventy percent of the adolescents showed their largest I–V difference on the first or second block pairs (comparison of block 1 with 2 or block 3 with 4), rather than during the final block pair, implying habituation of the ERP response to discrepancy. However, more high than low reactives (61% vs. 39%) showed their largest I–V difference on the final block pair, implying a shallower habituation to the invalid pictures ($\chi^2(1) = 4.6, p < .05$).

The magnitude of Wave 5 gathered at age 11 was related to the I–V difference on the final block pair, but not to the I–V differences on the first two block pairs ($r = .34, p < .05$). Eighty-five percent of the adolescents with an I–V difference greater than the mean on the final block pair had Wave 5 values greater than the mean at age 11 (12 of 14); whereas only 33% with small I–V differences had a large Wave 5 ($\chi^2 = 9.1, p < .01$). Eight high reactives (three boys and five girls from a group of 27), but only one low reactive, with a large I–V difference on the final block pair also had large Wave 5 values at 11 years, and seven of these eight high reactives had large Wave 5 values at age 15. This profile implies a special brain state and these eight high-reactive adolescents displayed unique features. Two high-reactive boys often avoided looking at the interviewer and four other high reactives reported atypical fears during the interview. One boy was afraid of a terrorist attack, one girl was anxious when she thought she might be touched, a third worried about planned school trips to unfamiliar places, and a fourth told the interviewer, "I feel vulnerable when I'm with people I don't know because I don't know what to do or say." The remaining two from the group of eight were high-reactive girls who were clinically depressed and under psychiatric care. Thus, every one of the eight high reactives with large values for Wave 5 at age 11 and relatively shallow habituation of the N400 waveform to the invalid pictures displayed either extreme uncertainty or a seriously depressed mood. Not one low reactive displayed this combination of features.

RESULTS

Frontal Asymmetry of the N400

Larger I–V differences were associated with larger integrated voltages at F4 (right frontal area) than at F3 (left frontal area), a result that is expected because the stimuli were pictures. Among the adolescents whose largest I–V difference on any block pair was greater than the median value for the entire sample, 65% had larger values at F4 than F3 (by at least 1 μV). By contrast, among adolescents whose largest I–V difference was smaller than the median, only 25% had larger values at F4 than at F3 ($\chi^2 = 6.2$, $p < .01$). In addition, the larger the resting EEG asymmetry value favoring left frontal activation, the smaller the N400 values to the final block of invalid pictures ($r = .43$, $p < .05$). Thus, a bias that favored left frontal activation at rest was associated with more rapid habituation to the invalid pictures, especially among the low reactives. Nine of 10 low reactives whose largest I–V difference occurred on the first block pair were left frontal active at rest, compared with two of seven low reactives whose largest I–V difference was on the final block pair ($p < .05$ by the Exact Test).

A similar result emerged on the larger sample of 205 children on whom ERPs had been gathered at age 11 years. Recall that the 11-year-olds saw two series of pictures in an oddball paradigm with 169 pictures in each series. Fifteen percent of the pictures in the first series were ecologically valid, whereas 15% of the pictures in the second series were ecologically invalid. The 11-year-olds with larger voltages to the invalid than to the valid pictures had larger values at F4 than at F3; those with larger values to the valid scenes had larger values at F3 than at F4 (Kagan & Snidman, 2004).

N100 to the Pictures

The 15-year-olds showed a prominent negative waveform, usually larger at F4 than at F3, with a peak magnitude at about 140 m second and a range between 100 and 180 ms that probably represents the components of the N100 waveform (Naatanen & Picton, 1987).

Figure 3 illustrates the median values for the integrated voltages from 100 to 180 ms to the valid and invalid pictures across each of the six blocks. Because the values at F4 were consistently higher than those at F3 we analyzed the F4 values (see Figure 3). We determined which adolescents showed a linear decrease in magnitude of the N100 across the three blocks of invalid pictures, compared with those showing no change or an increase in voltage across blocks. Thirty-seven percent of low reactives, but only 18% of high reactives, showed a linear decrease in the magnitude of this early waveform. By contrast, 16% of low reactives but 52% of high reactives showed no change or an increase in voltage over the three blocks of invalid pictures ($\chi^2 = 7.6$, $p < .01$).

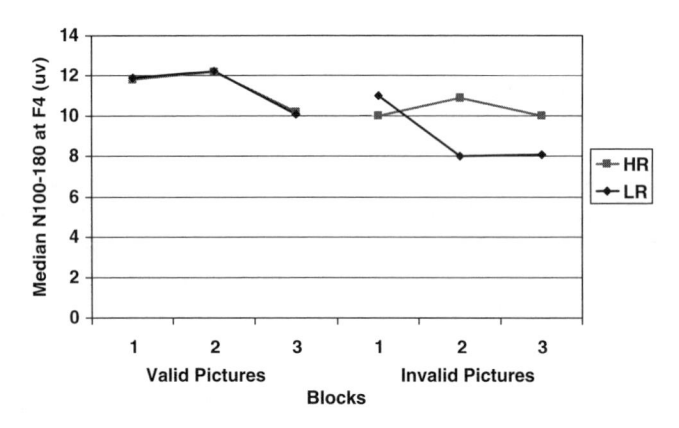

![Figure 3 chart showing Median N100-180 at F4 (uv) across blocks of Valid Pictures (1-3) and Invalid Pictures (1-3) for HR and LR groups]

FIGURE 3.—The N100 waveform to the blocks of valid and invalid pictures for high and low reactives.

Finally, for 77% of low reactives, compared with 35% of high reactives, the largest values on the final block pair were responses to the valid rather than the invalid pictures for both the early (N100) and later (N400) waveforms. By contrast, 65% of high reactives, but 23% of low reactives, had their largest values for both waveforms on the final block pair to the invalid scenes ($\chi^2(1) = 10.3, p < .01$). Thus, high reactives showed shallower habituation of both the N100 and N400 waveforms to the invalid scenes.

N400 to the Incongruous Sentences

A repeated measures analysis of variance on the integrated voltages from 350 to 450 ms for the 40 valid and 40 invalid sentences failed to reveal a significant F for sentence validity or temperament, even though the voltages were higher for invalid than for valid sentences.

Cardiovascular Profiles

The ratio of power in the higher frequency band ($\geq .2$ Hz) over the power in the lower frequency band (.05–.15 Hz), computed from the spectral analysis of each adolescent's supine heart rate, did not separate the temperamental groups at age 15 although this variable did so at age 11 years. The ratio of low over high power was stable from 11 to 15 years for boys ($r = .60, p < .05$) but not for girls ($r = -.10$). Resting heart rate also failed to separate the temperamental categories, even though it, too, was stable from 11 to 15 years for both sexes ($r = .36, p < .05$ for boys; $r = .53, p < .01$ for girls). However, 7 of 18 low-reactive boys, but only one of 14 high-reactive boys showed spectral ratios greater than the median (reflecting vagal tone) and resting heart rates greater than the median at both

11 and 15 years of age. By contrast, five high-reactive boys, but only two low-reactive boys, showed ratios less than the median and heart rates greater than the median at both ages ($p < .05$ by the Exact Test). As was true at age 11, only low-reactive boys displayed greater vagal tone than high-reactive boys at 15 years of age. These variables did not separate the high- and low-reactive girls.

Although there was no significant temperament difference in mean systolic or diastolic blood pressure (sitting or standing), higher sitting systolic blood pressure was associated with the rating of inhibition during the interview for high-reactive boys ($r = .62$, $p < .05$). Further, the magnitude of increase in heart rate from a sitting to a standing posture was larger than predicted for high- than for low-reactive boys (based on regression of the change in heart rate on standing over the sitting value); 76% of high reactives but only 36% of low reactives had a larger than predicted increase in heart rate ($\chi^2(1) = 5.8$, $p < .05$). There were no significant differences in mean systolic or diastolic blood pressure under a sitting or standing posture.

A final unexpected result warrants mention. It will be recalled that more high than low reactives confessed to being worried over unfamiliar people, situations, or the future. Because this target of concern could be potentiated by afferent feedback from the cardiovascular system, we examined the relation between systolic blood pressure and reporting that performance, on the one hand, or unfamiliarity, on the other, was a source of worry. We used the 11-year-old systolic values in order to maximize the sample size. The stability correlation for sitting systolic blood pressure from 11 to 15 years was .3 ($p < .05$). The adolescents who nominated unfamiliarity or the future as a source of worry on at least one of the three interview questions had significantly higher sitting systolic blood pressure at age 11 compared with those who only nominated performance ($F_{(1, 111)} = 4.83$, $p < .05$). There was no effect of temperament or gender and no interaction.

V. DISCUSSION

This assessment of 15-year-olds classified as high or low reactive at 4 months has affirmed only some of the results found at earlier ages. High reactives continued to differ from low reactives in degree of affective spontaneity in unfamiliar social situations. More high than low reactives, at every assessment, from 14 months to 15 years, were motorically tense and smiled infrequently, whereas more low reactives were relaxed and smiled often. These behavioral differences were clearer for boys than for girls at 15 years. Second, high reactives described themselves as less sanguine and more dour than low reactives. However, the small number of high-reactive adolescents who reported a sanguine mood, especially those who were religious, relied primarily on a concordance between their ethical standards for the qualities of a good person and their accomplishments. By contrast, low reactives who reported a sanguine mood seemed to rely primarily on their internal feeling tone as referent. Plato and Aristotle would probably have agreed with the definition of happy held by the high reactives because of their view that eudaimonia—a special quality of happiness—is attained through a rational control of impulse that allows each person to live a virtuous life (Yu & Gracia, 2003). It should be noted, however, that low reactive adolescents are not under-controlled or impulsive; they simply have a higher threshold of reactivity to uncertainty.

Although the two temperamental groups continued to differ in asymmetry of activation in the EEG, magnitude of Wave 5, rate of habituation of the ERP to discrepant visual scenes, and sympathetic or vagal tone in the cardiovascular system, these differences were much less dramatic at age 15 than they were at age 11. As a result statistical significance was only seen when we combined the evidence at both ages. The reason for the less pronounced differences between adolescents originally classified as high versus low reactive is not clear. One possibility is that puberty is accompanied by both biological and psychological changes that enhance the control of the frontal cortex.

It is also unclear why the ERP wave forms to the invalid pictures separated the high from the low reactives better than the waveforms to the semantically incongruent sentences. One possibility is that the invalid pictures recruited a more vigorous surprise reaction than the invalid sentences. A second interpretation argues that the high reactives may be more susceptible to discrepant visual events than to semantic incongruity, and this distinction is honored by the brain. This is consistent with evidence that the parahippocampal gyrus is preferentially activated by discrepant scenes; whereas the perirhinal cortex is preferentially activated by semantic dissonance (O'Kane, Insler, & Wagner, 2005).

The complete corpus of evidence supports the hypothesis that the two temperamental types vary in threshold of amygdalar activation to unfamiliarity, which we suspect is due to the inheritance of different neurochemical profiles in the amygdala and, perhaps, other sites. One possible candidate, among many, is the effectiveness of GABA-ergic processes in the central nucleus of the amygdala. Unpublished research conducted in collaboration with Kevin Nugent revealed that the small number of newborns who cried so intensely they could not be soothed during a standard newborn examination were most likely to be classified as high reactive at 4 months. The failure to regulate extreme levels of distress during the opening days of life may imply a compromise in the inhibitory functions of GABA and/or its receptors.

This speculation should be viewed in connection with the finding, at both ages 11 and 15, that relations among and between the contemporary behavioral and biological measures were usually low and insignificant. The most behaviorally inhibited high reactive 15-year-old boy was left frontal active, had a small Wave 5, a small I–V difference, and more vagal than sympathetic tone. A low-reactive girl who described herself as melancholic on the Q-sort and told the interviewer she worried about the future showed left frontal activation, a small Wave 5, a small I–V difference, but greater sympathetic than vagal tone.

SOURCES OF WORRY

High and low reactives at age 15 differed more markedly in their self-reported worries and moods than in their observed behaviors with the interviewer or the laboratory examiner. More high than low reactives reported serious concern over future encounters with the unfamiliar and confessed to frequent melancholic moods. At the same time, some high-reactive youth (boys as well as girls) with this affect profile were not unusually subdued or shy during the interview, nor did these adolescents report timidity in their social encounters. Their social behavior was dissociated from their private feelings—a phenomenon that may be related to maturation of frontal, executive functions with a corresponding increase in abilities to control public acts (see similar result in Willinger & Aschauer, 2005).

The adolescents' descriptions of their worries point to the importance of distinguishing between realistic and less realistic concerns. Inadequate performance at school, or on the athletic field or stage, constitute realistic concerns with relatively clear features. Most youths know their level of talent, know the qualities of their performances that will be evaluated, understand that poor school performance can affect their vocational future, and appreciate that study and practice can decrease the probability of obtaining a grade or athletic performance less adequate than the one they desire. Further, the likelihood of complete school failure is low in this middle-class, conscientious sample. These realistic worries are marked by minimal ambiguity and adolescents' knowledge that they have some control over the outcome. As a result, the level of uncertainty is muted to some degree.

By contrast, future encounters with strangers, new places, or novel challenges have more ambiguous features, the ability to control the outcome is compromised, and serious failure is possible. The adolescents reporting these worries are unsure of the personal qualities others will judge, how they will react, and believe there is not much they can do to reduce the probability of awkward or inappropriate behaviors. Therefore, the level of uncertainty in these youth is higher than the level experienced by those concerned only with performance. One prototypic, high-reactive adolescent girl, who had been very inhibited at 14 months, told the interviewer she does not like spring because of the unpredictable changes in weather. A high-reactive boy reported feeling anxious in dyadic interactions because he was aware of all the alternative things he could say and was uncertain as to which statements would be interpreted as undesirable.

This distinction between worry over an adequate performance and worry over encountering new people, places, and challenges, which resembles Freud's contrast between realistic and neurotic anxiety, is supported by others (Fisher et al., 2006; Laugesen, Dugas, & Bukowski, 2003). For example, a survey of the fears of college students from seven different societies revealed no significant cultural or gender differences in the incidence of realistic fears of dangerous animals (tigers or sharks), but significant cultural and sex differences in the incidence of less realistic fears of small animals, such as cockroaches, worms, and rats (Davey et al., 1998). The small group of young accountants working in large firms who regarded their role assignment as ambiguous and a major source of worry reported bringing their uncertainty from the workplace to their home (Doby & Caplan, 1995).

DISCUSSION

Adults classified as high in anxiety sensitivity reported a heightened concern over future events they could not control (Floyd, Garfield, & La Sota, 2005), and more intense, unpleasant affect during the first few minutes of a carbon dioxide challenge (the subjects were breathing 10% CO_2 enriched air) (Feldner et al., 2006). A large sample of middle-class adults with a diagnosis of social phobia contained two different sub-groups separated by the realistic nature of their fears. The patients who were anxious over meeting strangers reported anhedonia and a depressed mood; the group anxious over the quality of their public performances reported high levels of physiological arousal (Hughes et al., 2006). The amygdala is activated more consistently by unfamiliar events than by possible failure (Hsu et al., 2005; Rozin & Cohen, 2003). That is probably why individuals in an induced state of cognitive uncertainty showed activation of the areas to which the amygdala sends projections, especially the medial prefrontal cortex, ventral striatum, and anterior insula (Grinband, Hirsch, & Ferrera, 2006).

The self-reported fears of monozygotic twins and their spouses characterized by a low probability of harm (e.g., an accident while boating or walking in a dark place) had significantly higher heritability values than the occurrence of realistic fears of illness, an automobile accident, task failure, or criticism for a mistake (Sundet et al., 2003). This last result suggests that inherited temperamental biases have a greater influence on the intensity and frequency of less realistic, improbable threats, and might explain why individuals with social anxiety overestimate the frequency of angry faces presented in a long series that included both happy and neutral faces (Garner, Mogg, & Bradley, 2006).

VULNERABILITY TO VISCERAL FEEDBACK

All adolescents meet new people, visit unfamiliar places, and can neither know nor control future events. Thus, we must ask why high reactives were more likely than low reactives to name these events as primary sources of worry. One possible answer is that they are more susceptible to spontaneous visceral feedback, especially from targets of the autonomic nervous system, that pierces consciousness and creates uncertainty because it is unpredicatable and its origin ambiguous. This feeling of uncertainty shares features with the state evoked when children encounter unfamiliar objects, people, or situations. Because the amygdala participates in both states, it is possible that the state created by the unexpected visceral feedback functions as a conditioned stimulus to provoke the earlier state of uncertainty that accompanied encounters with unfamiliarity. Stated differently, because the feeling generated by the unexpected visceral feedback is uncontrollable, and its origin ambiguous, it resembles the feeling evoked when the person anticipates a future encounter with strangers or new places.

Adults with larger evoked potentials in the prefrontal cortex, insula, and anterior cingulate (associated with the R-wave of a systole) are better able to detect their heartbeats (Pollatos, Karsch, & Schandry, 2005). If high reactives had larger evoked potentials to a systole, or possessed a prefrontal cortex that was less effective in modulating the amygdala (Price, 2005), they should have higher scores on measures of anxiety sensitivity (Bernstein et al., 2006) and, perhaps, social anxiety as well (see Eisenberger, Leiberman, & Satpute, 2005). A fear of tachycardia, respiratory distress, inability to concentrate, and display of signs of anxiety to others—called anxiety sensitivity—should be regarded as a qualitative category, rather than a continuum. About 15–20% of young adults from six different countries fit this category (Bernstein et al., 2006). Recall that about 20% of the infants in our sample were high reactive.

The suggestion that anticipation of a novel event can evoke associations created in the past under a state of uncertainty is supported by research with animals. A large sample of 3-month-old rats experienced a single electric shock, an unexpected event that would have activated the amygdala, when they stepped down from an elevated platform onto a grid. Subgroups of animals were tested subsequently at varied intervals to determine how long they delayed before stepping off the platform. Animals exposed to a harmless, but novel, environment 1 hour before being placed on the platform retained their memory of the original shock experience for 19 months. By contrast, rats not exposed to the novel environment showed no behavioral evidence of a memory for the original event (Izquierdo et al., 2003). This intriguing result implies that memories of salient childhood events that created uncertainty can be triggered by anticipations of, or encounters with other, quite different, sources of uncertainty.

High-reactive youth in our culture are biased to interpret the feeling evoked by visceral feedback as implying that they are worried about their ability to cope with a future novel encounter because strangers and new places are the most frequent novelties in their lives, and the folk theory they have learned implies that their feelings of uncertainty are due to a compromise in their psychological characteristics. Members of other cultures might impose different interpretations on the same visceral feedback. Cambodian refugees living in Massachusetts interpret an unexpected bout of tachycardia as implying a weak heart caused by a loss of energy following lack of sleep or a diminished appetite (Hinton et al., 2005a, 2005b). We remind readers that our sample is composed of middle-class, Caucasian children and it remains a possibility that samples from different class or ethnic groups might produce different results.

Kindling

If unexpected visceral feedback, or intense uncertainty accompanying encounter with the unfamiliar, were frequent experiences during childhood, the amygdalahippocampal pathway could become permanently sensitized—the technical term is kindled—and such children could remain vulnerable to anxiety over anticipated unfamiliarity for a long time (Pape & Stork, 2003). Cambodian refugees who suffered severe trauma during the Pol Pot regime were vulnerable to occasional episodes of sleep paralysis accompanied by images and hallucinations of threatening figures (Hinton et al., 2005b). It is reasonable to assume that the earlier traumatic experiences kindled the amygdalae of some refugees, rendering them susceptible to spontaneous amygdalar discharge and activation of the neurons of the central gray responsible for body immobility to a threatening incentive.

Rat strains differ in the ease of amygdalar kindling due, in part, to inherited neurochemical profiles (Mohapel & McIntyre, 1998; Kelly et al., 2003). Oxytocin, which mutes excitatory flow from the amygdala to the brainstem, might be one candidate molecule (Huber, Veinante, & Stoop, 2005). Adults given oxytocin intranasally showed less activation of the amygdala to faces with fearful or angry expressions than individuals given a placebo (Kirsch et al., 2005). Hence, an inherited compromise in oxytocin function should render children more vulnerable to anxiety over the unfamiliar.

AN INTEGRATED PROPOSAL

We suggest that unexpected encounters with unfamiliar events, including unexpected visceral feedback, activate the locus ceruleus, amygdala, cingulate, and prefrontal cortex to create a unique brain state that can function as a conditioned stimulus capable of evoking a host of past representations possessing the same biological feature. Internal states can serve as conditioned stimuli in both rats and humans (De Grandpere, Bickel, & Higgins, 1992; Dekeyne & Millan, 2003; Servatius & Beck, 2005). When the senior author was jogging on the side of a country road in 1966 he twisted his ankle, had a vasovagal reaction, fell to the ground, and was unconscious for a few minutes. Twenty years later, when his ankle twisted only slightly while walking slowly on a different road, the memory of the earlier experience pierced consciousness immediately, implying that the incentive for the recalled memory was the brain state created by sensory feedback from the muscles of the slightly twisted ankle.

It is possible that encounters with the unfamiliar generate a more salient psychobiological state in high than low reactives because of their neurochemistry. This state is evoked when they think about a future encounter characterized by unfamiliarity. The psychological derivatives of this state are a conscious feeling of worry and a disposition to avoid the feared events. Although a feeling of anxiety can accompany realistic concern over a final examination or the less realistic concern over a visit to New York City for the first time, these worries might have different neurobiological foundations (Phelps, 2006). A rat's response to fox odor and to a conditioned stimulus for shock activate different genes and the behaviors accompanying each incentive are uncorrelated across or within rat strains (Rosen, Adamec, & Thompson, 2005).

If the sources of unfamiliarity were the colors, tastes, and viscosities of liquids with a bitter taste, rather than strangers or new places, high reactives might worry about drinking liquids with a novel color or viscosity, and psychiatrists would have created a category called "drinking phobia." Clinicians are familiar with patients who have phobias of unfamiliar foods, a phenomenon also found in animals. Social anxiety is more frequent in our culture than anxiety over drinking an unfamiliar liquid because strangers and new places are more common. Pious medieval Christians who suffered a misfortune after violating an ethical norm worried because they believed that their distress was caused by God's wrath. John Calvin, the strict Protestant reformer from Geneva, worried continually over God's disapproval of his actions (Bouwsma, 1984). The Saulteaux Indians of Manitoba worry about contracting a serious disease because illness implies violation of an ethical norm on sexual, aggressive, or sharing behavior (Hallowell, 1941).

Social anxiety is a natural phenomenon, but it is especially salient in societies, like our own, where encounters with strangers and new places are frequent sources of uncertainty, and social acceptance is a primary goal. Temperaments can render individuals especially vulnerable to some member of the emotional family called anxiety; history and culture supply the specific target of this family. In contemporary America occupational and social failure have replaced the seven traditional sins of pride, anger, envy, avarice, sloth, gluttony, and lust as bases for anxiety or guilt.

Segments of a society can become vulnerable to anxiety over the validity of their ethical beliefs when historical changes in economy or demography alter the certainty of traditional norms and motivate those wishing to remain loyal to the older mores to support a counter-reformation that restores the traditional ideology. The witch craze in 15th century Europe was brought on, in part, by the desire among some citizens to restore women, who were beginning to enter the workforce, to their traditional roles as homemakers and mothers. Ideological uncertainty can, in certain contexts, lead to increased violence, especially when there is group support and citizens agree on who is responsible for their uncertainty. Hitler took advantage of this dynamic. Gould (2003) notes that homicides in Corsica peaked during periods of political unrest when an individual's social position became ambiguous.

New ideas with ethical implications are as powerful incentives for human anxiety or anger as unexpected or unfamiliar events are for animals, but we suspect that the physiological mechanisms are different. Worry over the abortions performed on unmarried adolescents does not require the basolateral nucleus of the amygdala; a rat's acquisition of conditioned freezing to a stimulus that signaled electric shock does. Thus, scientists should not treat classically conditioned responses in animals as an appropriate model for all human anxieties (for a different view, see Mineka & Zimbarg, 2006, and Phelps, 2006). Classical conditioning of freezing or potentiated startle might be a good model for human phobias of animals or heights, but it is less likely to illuminate the reasons for anxiety over a trip to Europe, a party with strangers, or becoming ill because one violated an ethical imperative to share food with a relative.

The claim that unfamiliar and unexpected events create a distinct brain state may apply to other classes of experience. For example, it is possible that events that produce sensory pleasure (e.g., sweet foods, sexual stimulation, warmth when cold) generate a distinct brain state that involves the insular cortex and its projections. Perhaps that is why the semantic terms for love objects, sweet-tasting foods, and summer are closely associated. Similar arguments could be made for the events that (a) generate sensory states of displeasure (e.g., pain, bitter taste, the sight or smell of mutilated or rotting flesh) (Morrison et al., 2004); (b) accompany the anticipation of an uncertain but desirable goal; or (c) signal imminent physical harm, failure, or criticism (Schultz, 2006). Most languages have terms for the emotions that in English are named "joy," "disgust," "excitement," and "fear".

INTERACTIONS WITH GENDER

The relations among the variables differed occasionally as a function of gender, or a combination of temperament and gender. High systolic blood pressure, for example, only predicted inhibited interview behavior for high-reactive boys, not for girls. Low-reactive boys, but not low-reactive girls, were most likely to report being happier at age 15 than at age 11; high-reactive girls were far more spontaneous during the interview than high-reactive boys.

Other investigators have also found that gender interacts with the temperamental biases that contribute to personality types. The association between the DRD4 polymorphism and extraversion in African-American adults was significant for women, but not men (Bookman et al., 2002), and the association between respiratory or skin allergies and depression was strong for females but not for males (Timonen et al., 2003). Although men and women breathing 20% CO_2-enriched air showed equivalent changes in heart rate, skin conductance, and muscle tension, more women than men reported feelings of fear and symptoms of panic (Kelly, Forsyth, & Karekla, 2006). Women showed shallower habituation of amygdala activation to faces with fearful expressions than men (Williams et al., 2005), and women from different cultures reported more fears of small, harmless animals (worms, flies, and mice) than men (Arrindell et al., 2003). This last fact might reflect a sex difference in concern over contamination, rather than a fear of physical injury (Husted, Shapira, & Goodman, 2006). Many additional studies reinforce the claim that it is common for the relations among, or between, behavioral and biological variables to be different for males and females.

RISK FOR PSYCHOPATHOLOGY

The only adolescent male diagnosed with social anxiety disorder, who was under psychiatric care, had been a high-reactive infant who displayed frequent arches of the back and a chronically unhappy facial expression during the 4-month battery, as well as fear scores in the second year that were in the top quintile of the distribution. This boy screamed at 14 months when a stranger entered the playroom and, at 21 months, screamed when a blood pressure cuff was applied and when a clown unexpectedly opened the door of the playroom where he was playing. This boy missed many days during his senior year of high school because of extreme social anxiety. He reported that he feels "panicky" in crowds and was spending a great deal of time playing video games in his bedroom. However, rather than present a timid persona, he was an angry young man who peppered his interview replies with obscenities. This youth had adopted a rebellious self-presentation that denied guilt, moments of happiness, and any hope for his future. This boy's longitudinal record invites the conclusion that his high-reactive temperament made a substantial contribution to his current mood and personality profile. It is probably not a coincidence that college students who reported an intolerance of uncertainty (e.g., they endorsed statements such as "My mind is not relaxed if I don't know what will happen") reported frequent and intense worries on a questionnaire (Buhr & Dugas, 2006).

Although high reactives are more likely than others to become shy adults, most will not develop a diagnosis of social phobia. Only one of every two adults in the 90th percentile for self-reported shyness were diagnosed as social phobics (Chavira, Stein, & Malcarne, 2002), and less than 50% of chronically shy children developed the psychiatric symptoms that define social anxiety disorder (Biederman et al., 2001; Prior, Smart, Sanson, & Oberklaid, 2000). Further, about one-half of adults diagnosed with social phobia reported that they did not remember being excessively shy as young children, although they might have distorted the memories of their childhood personalities (Cox, McPherson, & Enns, 2005).

It is possible to change the behaviors of adolescents diagnosed with social anxiety. A 12-week school-based intervention with adolescents who had social phobia reduced the level of social anxiety in two-thirds of the youth (Masia-Warner et al., 2005). These facts are in accord with animal work implying that the amygdala links a conditioned stimulus with the sensory features of an unconditioned stimulus, whereas the orbitofrontal cortex links the conditioned stimulus to an operant response (Holland & Gallagher, 2004), suggesting that the overt behavioral profile displayed by unfamiliarity is malleable, even though the vulnerability to uncertainty is preserved.

Serious depression, although infrequent in our sample, occurred more often among high than low reactives. Five of the nine cases of clinical depression under psychiatric care had been high-reactive girls (the other four included one low-reactive girl and three girls from the other temperamental group). A longitudinal study of over 500 Canadian children, ages 6–14, revealed that the small number of adolescents who showed an increase in depressed mood from 11 to 14 years were girls who had been described by their mothers as unusually reactive to frustration, pain, or disappointment when they were 6 years old (Brendgen et al., 2005).

A small number of high-reactive girls developed both anxiety to the unfamiliar and a depressed mood. One of many possible explanations of this fact is less effective binding of the serotonin transporter within the amygdala, a condition that would be associated with greater amygdalar activity. Adults with one or both of the short alleles of 5-HTTLPR showed greater activity in the right amygdala to unexpected presentation of fearful or angry faces (Hariri, Drabant, & Weinberger, 2006). Another research team reported that depressed adults, who had never taken antidepressants, possessed a lower binding potential of the serotonin transporter within the amygdala (Parsey et al., 2006b); however, this compromise was not related to possession of the short polymorphism in the promoter region of the 5-HTTLPR gene (Parsey et al., 2006a).

It is a speculative possibility that the neurochemistry of high reactives might interfere with the intensity of the subjective state of "pleasure" that often occurs when a person receives, or anticipates receiving, an unexpected or larger than anticipated desired experience. This state is mediated, in part, by the discharge of dopamine producing neurons accompanying the anticipation of a desired event (Fiorillo, Tobler, & Schultz, 2003; Schultz, 2006). Further, CRH neurons, which are usually activated by the anticipation of threat, and are present in dopamine-producing brain sites, can suppress the release of dopamine to an imminent reward (Austin, Rhodes, & Lewis, 1997). Several laboratories have reported an association between introversion and polymorphisms of the COMT gene that affect the efficiency of dopamine degradation in the synapse (Stein et al., 2005; Reuter & Hennig, 2005; Golimbet et al., 2005).

Perhaps one reason why high-reactive adolescents do not like novel or risky activities, even though they promise the pleasure of excitement, is that they fail to experience pleasure when they anticipate visiting a new city, meeting a new person, or engaging in a new activity, and more often experience an unpleasant feeling. This profile should make them risk averse to novelty, rather than motivate the seeking of new events (Netter, 2006). This argument finds support in a study of 111 college students who had initially filled out a questionnaire measuring social anxiety, and later rated their moods on 21 consecutive days. The students with high scores on the social anxiety scale were least likely to report pleasurable experiences, and often reported a melancholic mood, across the 21 days (Kashdan & Steger, 2006).

Fear Versus Disgust

It is likely that fear of harm and disgust, two states associated with avoidance, are mediated by different neurophysiologies. Worry over being harmed or attacked by some external agent usually involves vision and hearing, the basolateral amygdala, sympathetic nervous system, ventral striatum, and central gray. This combination is the flee or fight system provoked by threatening external events, or their anticipation, and is linked to a semantic network whose nodes are fear, anxiety, and danger. By contrast, worry over being contaminated by particular objects or animals, probably derived from earlier experiences with unpleasant tastes and smells, involves the olfactory and gustatory cortex, feelings of discomfort from the gut, anterior insular cortex, central nucleus of the amygdala, and parasympathetic nervous system (Fitzgerald et al., 2004). This combination is linked to a semantic network whose nodes are disgust, polluted, defiled, and contaminated.

This distinction could explain why factor analyses of self-reported fears usually reveal distinct factors for events that can injure the body, such as large animals and airplane flights, and events that can contaminate, such as worms, mice, and spiders. Pictures of human injury due to aggression, compared with pictures of dirty toilets, elicit different γ band profiles (Oya et al., 2002).

Bitter or sour tastes, the pungent smell of hydrogen sulfide, and a stomach-ache activate the insular cortex automatically, and do not require knowledge of their meaning or symbolic significance. Activation of the amygdala by a dagger, snake, tiger, or gun requires knowledge of their potential danger, which the amygdala receives from the entorhinal and parahippocampal cortices. Although the amygdala and the anterior insula are reciprocally connected, the latter site elaborates the information from the former, and the two structures are modulated by different neurochemistries. Hence, it is reasonable to expect that individuals will vary in the targets of their fears. This expectation is affirmed by the fact that the biological features of patients with phobias of dangerous animals are different from the biological features of patients, many diagnosed with OCD, who fear contamination from worms, mice, or spiders (Fitzgerald et al., 2004). Most of our high reactives did not report fears of insects, rats, or mice. Their fears emphasized unfamiliar experiences they could not prepare for in advance and a frequent coping strategy was an attempt to control the future, which occasionally took the form of perfectionism and compulsive rituals. These emotions are more likely to be mediated by an excitable amygdala than by an aroused insula.

AMBIGUITY OF SINGLE MEASUREMENTS

The current data, along with the results of others, imply that single variables rarely have a univocal meaning. For example, left or right frontal activation represents only one component of a brain state that is integrated with other features of the person's biology, past experience, and the local context to create one of many possible psychological states. Left frontal activation does not represent or predict an "approach tendency" in most individuals, independent of their temperament and gender (Coan & Allen, 2004). One research team reported that many adolescent patients with serious mood and behavior disorders displayed left, rather than right, frontal activation (Rybak et al., 2006). High-functioning autistic children with left frontal activation reported more social anxiety than those who showed right frontal activation (Sutton et al., 2005). College students asked to self-induce a state of worry over public speaking showed the expected decrease in heart rate variability and increase in self-reported distress, but, surprisingly, there was no change in direction of asymmetry of frontal or parietal activation. Most participants were left frontal active during both the baseline and the mood induction intervals (Hofmann et al., 2005). The eight women with a phobia of spiders (from a larger group of phobics) who had a panic attack while watching a film of live spiders showed a decrease, rather than an increase, in the magnitude of right frontal activation (Johanson et al., 1998). The self-reported emotional state following amobarbital induced anesthesia of one hemisphere varied with the individual's personality and the ambience of the test situation (Stabell et al., 2004). The profiles of brain activation evoked by faces with surprise or fearful expressions also varied across individuals (Kim et al., 2004; Moriguchi et al., 2005), and similar brain profiles to erotic or disgusting scenes were accompanied by distinctly different ratings of level of arousal (Stark et al., 2005).

It is generally the case that the psychological significance, or behavioral consequences, of most emotional incentives can not be confidently inferred from the pattern of brain activity the incentives provoked because the brain's response is influenced not only by the physical features, familiarity, and expectedness of the events, but also by its personal meaning for the individual (Kim et al., 2004). Each brain state can be the foundation of a number of psychological states, depending on the individual's past history and the local context (Balaban, Alper, & Kasamon, 1996). The pattern of brain activity in the anterior cingulate to a painful thermal stimulus, for example, depended on whether self or another person administered the painful event (Mohr et al., 2005; see also Rollnik, Schmitz, & Kugler, 2001). Major theoretical advances will follow the invention of terms for the varied brain states that are currently given psychological names.

Our evidence also illustrated the ambiguity of verbal replies to questions as simple as: "Are you happy most of the time?" or "Does your heart rate increase when you speak in front of the class?" Because these self-reports had different correlates in low and high reactives, it is likely that reports of more complex psychological states are equally ambiguous, and investigators should not treat similar answers to a question as having the same transparent meaning (Schienle et al., 2006).

Recall that the maternal descriptions of our adolescents when they were 11 years old did not predict their behavior in the interview or their Q-sorts at age 15, whereas their infant temperament did. Eighteen high-reactive adolescents were extremely inhibited during the interview, compared with only three low reactives, but their mothers had described 11 of these 18 as being uninhibited when they were 11 years old. Thus the constructs inferred from parental descriptions should be given a conceptual name different from the ones used to describe observed behavior.

Adults instructed to worry about issues they had previously told the investigator were serious sources of concern showed activation of frontal sites (measured by PET), but less activity in the amygdala and the insula, and no change in heart rate or skin conductance. This result suggests that their self-reports of worry, produced by brooding about personal issues, were primarily cognitive judgments (Hoehn-Saric et al., 2005). Japanese patients who complained of chronic somatic discomfort (e.g., chest pain, fatigue, tension headache) reported higher levels of tension to a cognitive stress than controls but, surprisingly, displayed lower levels of muscle tension and skin conductance (Kanbara et al., 2004). In addition, stroke patients with lesions in the right or left hemisphere, which should have compromised the ability to experience an emotion, correctly named the emotions of faces displaying fear, anger, sadness, or disgust (Braun et al., 2005). Finally, although the brain activation profiles induced by the initial exposure to faces displaying fear or disgust were dramatically reduced when adults saw them a week later, their subjective ratings of arousal were unchanged (Stark et al., 2003). All of this evidence implies that investigators cannot assume that a verbal report of an emotional state reflects the same biological or psychological state in all respondents offering the same verbal description (see Stark et al., 2005).

A single variable, like the meaning of the word "missed" in a sentence, does not have a univocal theoretical meaning because most self-reports, behaviors, or physiological reactions can be the product of more than one set of conditions. This conclusion is especially relevant for the popular constructs "fear" or "anxiety" when applied to animals and humans. Rats with preconditioning lesions in different brain structures experienced electric shock in one distinctive chamber and no shock in an equally distinctive chamber. The animals were then placed, on different occasions, in either the shock or safe chamber while several variables presumed to be indicative of a fear state were measured. The rats with lesions of the fornix (which mediates input to and output from the hippocampus) showed equivalent freezing, ultrasonic vocalizations, and defecation in the shock and safe chambers, implying that they were not very fearful. However, the same animals showed more urination and a higher heart rate when in the shock chamber, suggesting that they were fearful (Antoniadis & McDonald, 2006). Investigators who coded vocalization and freezing would have concluded that the lesioned rats were not fearful; those who quantified urination and heart rate would have concluded that they were fearful.

A second example involves the elevated maze. Many behavioral biologists assume that an animal's failure to enter the brightly lit area of an elevated maze reflects a state of "anxiety" in a mouse or rat. However, this conclusion is open to criticism. One research team compared the behaviors of rats, who had varied on a prior occasion in their exploration of the lit areas of an elevated maze, as they underwent classical Pavlovian conditioning with electric shock as the unconditioned stimulus. The animals who had failed to explore the lit areas on earlier tests emitted more ultrasonic vocalizations during Pavlovian conditioning than the animals who had explored the lit portions of the maze. This result implies that the prior failure to explore the lit areas might reflect the same state of anxiety present during conditioning. However, no rat emitted ultrasonic vocalizations in the elevated maze (Borta, Wohr, & Schwarting, 2006). If rats being conditioned with electric shock are presumed to be in an anxious state because they emitted vocalizations, the fact that they did not vocalize when in the maze suggests that their psychological state in the maze was different and the rats who avoided the lit areas were in a different state.

It is likely that the observations that comprise the foundations of many currently popular psychological constructs, not only fear or anxiety, have more than one set of causal conditions. A person might be classified as impulsive, for example, because of a life history that produced minimal concern with quality of performance or a biology that produced a compromise in frontal lobe function. A prolonged period of apathy could be provoked by loss of a loved one or a neurochemistry characterized by a compromise in norepinephrine function. However, self-reported feelings are unlikely to reveal these two conditions because most individuals find it difficult to differentiate between the feeling of apathy produced by a serious loss or an inherited neurochemistry. Similarly, most adolescents or adults can not discriminate between the quality of worry generated by anticipated failure on an examination and worry over a trip to Europe provoked by spontaneous bouts of visceral feedback. Two photographs of the Washington Monument, one made with traditional film and the other with a digital camera, appear very similar despite the distinctly different mechanisms producing the two pictures.

THE ROMANCE WITH BIOLOGY

Most scientists acknowledge that complex psychological profiles, such as social anxiety, depression, and violent behavior, are a joint function of a biologically based diathesis and a set of experiences. Hence, it is appropriate to ask why there is more enthusiasm and financial suppport for research probing the biological, rather than the environmental, contributions to these profiles when the priorities were reversed a half-century earlier. There are several reasons for the current bias.

First, most natural scientists prefer materialistic explanations of phenomena. Genes, neurons, transmitters, and circuits are material entities whose forms can be observed or imagined, whereas feelings and thoughts do not have this property. Hence, the suggestion that the chemical changes that accompany conditioned gill withdrawal in the sea snail Aplysia share features with human anxiety states is appealing (Kandel, 1983). Second, anxiety, mood disorders, and criminality are more common among those who are poor and/or belong to an ethnic minority. Therefore, investigators who reported that parental practices contributed to these symptoms might provoke the accusation that they held a prejudicial attitude toward the socially disadvantaged. It is politically incorrect to blame the victim.

Third, theoretical advances in every science often follow the invention of new, more powerful methods. Investigators interested in the influence of the environment on humans continue to use the traditional methods of questionnaires, interviews, or behavioral observations, and have not developed more powerful ways to measure the psychological consequences of experience. By contrast, geneticists, molecular biologists, and neuroscientists enjoy many novel technologies that became available over the past 2 or 3 decades. Some of these methods are more easily implemented with rats and mice than with humans. Hence, investigators seeking research funds, as well as acceptance from colleagues, rationalize the use of rodents as a useful model for human mental illnesses. These investigators typically probe the biological, rather than the environmental, contributions to a behavioral outcome. However, there is no experimental manipulation with mice that could simulate the effects of being an economically disadvantaged member of an ethnic minority, a homely child rejected by peers, or a parent who believes that her negligence was responsible for her infant's death.

We are skeptical of the claim that the genetic and physiological features that mediate a mouse's avoidance of the brightly lit areas of an elevated maze will account for most pathological forms of anxiety in humans. Psychologists who were committed to behaviorism 50 years ago rationalized studies of rats learning the correct turns in mazes as a useful model for the acquisition of human competences, such as language and reading. History has not been kind to that premise. Thus, materialism, a reluctance to blame the victim, and powerful biological techniques that can be used more effectively with animals than humans came together to create the current imbalance in the study of the causes of variation in human psychopathology and personality.

This imbalance was present in a recent paper reporting that, among English-speaking respondents 18 years and older, the lifetime prevalence for anxiety disorders was 28.8% and for mood disorders 20.8% (Kessler et al., 2005). This claim, similar to epidemiological reports of the prevalence of Huntingtons disease or Williams syndrome, implies, without stating so explicitly, that the pathophysiological bases for anxiety and mood disorders lie primarily within the patients, rather than in profound interactions between the biology of individuals, which are potentially measurable, and their past histories and current social settings, which are more difficult to quantify. Rather than report a national prevalence of 20% for anxiety disorders, investigators should present the prevalence rates for groups defined by their social class, ethnicity, and, perhaps, region of the country, for depression is, and has always been, more common among the urban poor than the rural rich (Weich, Twigg, & Lewis, 2006).

Nineteenth century European scholars, obsessed with social statistics, suggested that the year-to-year stability in the frequency of suicides and criminal acts implied that individuals who took their own or another's life were not completely responsible for their behaviors because they were obeying statistical laws (Hacking, 1990). Although the current biological perspective has great value, it has two disadvantages. The emphasis on biological causation diverts attention from the personal contributions to a patient's symptoms by those who interact with potential patients. Second, it motivates a single-minded approach to finding new drugs and psychotherapeutic treatments directed only at patients, rather than urging clinicians to combine these treatments with strategies that might alter the social context. Each river is capable of becoming polluted and losing its capacity to sustain life. However, ecologists do not attribute an inherent flaw to a river that has become polluted. Rather, they urge changes in the practices of industry and agriculture that are the root causes of the pollution. Psychiatrists and psychologists should adopt a similar strategy with anxiety and mood disorder.

SUMMARY

The central hypothesis proposed to explain the behavioral and biological differences between high and low reactives centers on distinct, but still unknown, neurochemistries that affect the excitability of limbic, and perhaps frontal cortex, sites to unexpected or unfamiliar events. The modest, but significant, differences in spontaneous social behavior, mood, asymmetry of frontal activation, Wave 5, sympathetic dominance in the cardiovascular system, and habituation of the event-related potential to discrepant visual events between 15-year-olds classified as high or low reactive at 4 months imply that the features that characterize these two temperamental biases are not completely malleable to the profound effects of brain growth and experience.

REFERENCES

Adamec, R. E., Blundell, J., & Burton, P. (2005a). Neural circuit changes mediating a lasting bias and behavioral response to predator stress. *Neuroscience and Biobehavioral Reviews*, **29**, 1225–1241.

Adamec, R. E., Blundell, J., & Burton, P. (2005b). Role of NMDA receptors in the lateralized potentiation of amygdala afferent and efferent neural transmission produced by predator stress. *Physiology and Behavior*, **86**, 75–91.

Anokhin, A. P., Heath, A. C., & Myers, E. (2006). Genetic and environmental influences on frontal EEG asymmetry: A twin study. *Biological Psychology*, **71**, 289–295.

Antoniadis, E. A., & McDonald, R. J. (2006). Fornix, medial prefrontal cortex, nucleus accumbens, and mediodorsal thalamic nucleus: Roles in a fear-based context discrimination task. *Neurobiology of Learning and Memory*, **85**, 71–85.

Arbelle, S., Benjamin, J., Golin, M., Kremer, I., Belmaker, R. H., & Ebstein, R. P. (2003). Relation of shyness in grade school children to the genotype for the long form of the serotonin transporter promoter region polymorphism. *American Journal of Psychiatry*, **160**, 671–676.

Arrindell, W. A., Eisemann, M., Richter, J., Oei, T. P., Caballo, V. E., van der Ende, J., & the Cultural Clinical Psychology Study Group. (2003). Phobic anxiety in 11 nations. Part 1: Dimensional constancy of the five-factor model. *Behavior Research and Therapy*, **41**, 461–479.

Asendorpf, J. B. (1989). Shyness as a final, pathway for two different kinds of inhibition. *Journal of Personality and Social Psychology*, **57**, 481–492.

Asendorpf, J. B. (1991). Development of inhibited children's coping with unfamiliarity. *Child Development*, **62**, 1460–1474.

Aston-Jones, G., & Bloom, F. E. (1981). Norepinephrine containing locus ceruleus neurons in behaving rats exhibit pronounced responses to non-noxious environmental stimuli. *Journal of Neuroscience*, **1**, 887–900.

Auerbach, J., Geller, V., Lezer, S., Shinwell, E., Belmaker, R. H., & Levin, J. (1999). Dopamine D4 receptor (D4DR) and serotonin transporter promoter (5-HTTLPR) polymorphisms in the determination of temperament in 2-month-old infants. *Molecular Psychiatry*, **4**, 369–373.

Auerbach, J. G., Benjamin, J., Faroy, M., Geller, V., & Ebstein, R. (2001). DRD4 related to infant attention and information processing: A developmental link to ADHD? *Psychiatric Genetics*, **11**, 31–35.

Austin, M. C., Rhodes, J. L., & Lewis, D. A. (1997). Differential distribution of corticotropin-releasing hormone immunoreactive axons in monoaminergic nuclei of the human brainstem. *Neuropsychopharmacology*, **17**, 326–341.

Baas, J. M., Milstein, J., Donlevy, M., & Grillon, C. (2006). Brainstem correlates of defensive states in humans. *Biological Psychiatry*, **59**, 588–593.

Balaban, E., Alper, J. S., & Kasamon, Y. L. (1996). Mean genes and the biology of aggression: A critical review of recent animal and human research. *Journal of Neurogenetics*, **11**, 1–43.

Barot, S. K., & Bernstein, I. L. (2005). Polycose taste pre-exposure fails to influence behavioral and neural indices of taste novelty. *Behavioral Neuroscience*, **119**, 1640–1647.

Bartels, M., van den Oord, E. J., Hudziak, J. J., Rietveld, M. J., van Beijsterveldt, C. E., & Boomsma, D. I. (2004). Genetic and environmental mechanisms underlying stability and change in problem behaviors at ages 3, 7, 10, and 12. *Developmental Psychology*, **40**, 852–867.

Bates, J. E. (1989). Concepts and measures of temperament. In J. A. Kohnstamm, J. E. Bates & M. K. Rothbart (Eds.), *Temperament and childhood* (pp. 3–26). New York: Wiley.

Battaglia, M., Ogliari, A., Zanoni, A., Citterio, A., Pozzoli, U., Giorda, R., Maffei, C., & Marino, C. (2005). Influence of the serotonin transporter promoter gene and shyness on children's cerebral responses to facial expressions. *Archives of General Psychiatry*, **62**, 85–94.

Benjamin, J., Osher, Y., Kotler, M., Gritsenko, I., Nemanov, L., Belmaker, R. H., & Ebstein, R. P. (2000). Association between tridimensional personality questionnaire (TPQ) traits and three functional polymorphisms: Dopamine receptor D4 (DRD4), serotonin transporter promoter region (5-HTTLPR) and catechol-O-methyltransferase (COMT). *Molecular Psychiatry*, **5**, 96–100.

Bernstein, A., Zvolensky, M. J., Kotov, R., Arrindell, W. A., Taylor, S., Sandin, B., Cox, B. J., Stewart, S. H., Bouvard, M., Cardenas, S. J., Eifert, G. H., & Schmidt, N. B. (2006). Taxonicity of anxiety sensitivity: A multi-national analysis. *Journal of Anxiety Disorders*, **20**, 1–22.

Bethea, C. L., Streicher, J. M., Coleman, K., Pau, F. K., Moessner, R., & Cameron, J. L. (2004). Anxious behavior and fenfluramine-induced prolactin secretion in young rhesus macaques with different alleles of the serotonin reuptake transporter polymorphism (5HTTLPR). *Behavior Genetics*, **34**, 295–307.

Bethea, C. L., Streicher, J. M., Mirkes, S. J., Sanchez, R. L., Reddy, A. P., & Cameron, J. L. (2005). Serotonin-related gene expression in female monkeys with individual sensitivity to stress. *Neuroscience*, **132**, 151–166.

Biederman, J., Hirshfeld-Becker, D. R., Rosenbaum, J. F., Herot, C., Friedman, D., Snidman, N., Kagan, J., & Faraone, S. V. (2001). Further evidence of association between behavioral inhibition and social anxiety in children. *American Journal of Psychiatry*, **158**, 1673–1679.

Bookman, E. B., Taylor, R. E., Adams-Campbell, L., & Kittles, R. A. (2002). DRD4 promoter snps and gender effects on extraversion in African Americans. *Molecular Psychiatry*, **7**, 786–790.

Bornas, X., Llabres, J., Noguera, M., Lopez, A. M., Barcelo, F., Tortella-Feliu, M., & Fullana, M. A. (2005). Looking at the heart of low and high heart rate variability fearful flyers: Self-reported anxiety when confronting feared stimuli. *Biological Psychology*, **70**, 182–187.

Borta, A., Wohr, M., & Schwarting, R. K. (2006). Rat ultrasonic vocalization in aversively motivated situations and the role of individual differences in anxiety-related behavior. *Behavioral Brain Research*, **166**, 271–280.

Bouwsma, W. J. (1984). John Calvin's anxiety. *The Proceedings of the American Philosophical Society*, **128**, 252–256.

Brandao, M. L., Coimbra, N. C., & Osaki, M. Y. (2001). Changes in the auditory-evoked potentials induced by fear-evoking stimulation. *Physiology and Behavior*, **72**, 365–372.

Braun, M., Traue, H. C., Frisch, S., Deighton, R. M., & Kessler, H. (2005). Emotion recognition in stroke patients with left and right hemispheric lesion: Results with a new instrument—the FEEL Test. *Brain and Cognition*, **58**, 193–201.

Brendgen, M., Wanner, B., Morin, A. J. S., & Vitaro, F. (2005). Relations with parents and with peers, temperament, and trajectories of depressed mood during early adolescence. *Journal of Abnormal Child Psychology*, **33**, 579–594.

Broberg, A., Lamb, M. E., & Hwang, P. (1990). Inhibition: Its stability and correlates in 16–40-month-old children. *Child Development*, **61**, 1153–1163.

Buhr, K., & Dugas, M. J. (2006). Investigating the construct validity of intolerance of uncertainty and its unique relationship with worry. *Journal of Anxiety Disorders*, **20**, 222–236.

Buss, K. A., Schumacher, J. R. M., Dolski, I., Kalin, N. H., Goldsmith, H. H., & Davidson, R. J. (2003). Right frontal brain activity, cortisol, and withdrawal behavior in 6-month-old infants. *Behavioral Neuroscience*, **117**, 11–20.

Caci, H., Robert, P., Dossios, C., & Boyer, P. (2005). Morningness–Eveningness for Children Scale: Psychometric properties and month of birth effect. *Encephale*, **31**, 56–64.

Cameron, O. G. (2002). *Visceral sensory neuroscience*. New York: Oxford University Press.

Carlsson, K., Petersson, K. M., Lundqvist, D., Karlsson, A., Ingvar, M., & Ohman, A. (2004). Fear and the amygdala: Manipulation of awareness generates differential cerebral responses to phobic and fear-relevant (but nonfeared) stimuli. *Emotion*, **4**, 340–353.

Cashdan, E. (1998). Smiles, speech, and body posture. *Journal of Nonverbal Behavior*, **22**, 209–228.

Caspi, A., Elder, G. H., & Bem, D. J. (1988). Living away from the world. *Developmental Psychology*, **24**, 824–831.

Caspi, A., McClay, J., Moffitt, T. E., Mill, J., Martin, J., Craig, I., Taylor, A., & Poulton, R. (2002). Evidence that the cycle of violence in maltreated children depends on genotype. *Science*, **297**, 851–854.

Caspi, A., & Silva, P. A. (1995). Temperamental qualities at age three predict personality traits in young adulthood. *Child Development*, **66**, 486–498.

Caspi, A., Sugden, K., Moffitt, T. E., Taylor, A., Craig, I. W., Harrington, H., McClay, J., Mill, J., Martin, J., Braithwaite, A., & Poulton, R. (2003). Influence of life stress on depression: Moderation by a polymorphism in the 5-HTT gene. *Science*, **301**, 386–389.

Castles, D. L., Whiten, A., & Aureli, F. (1999). Social anxiety, relationships and self-directed behaviour among wild female olive baboons. *Animal Behavior*, **58**, 1207–1215.

Chavira, D. A., Stein, M. B., & Malcarne, V. L. (2002). Scrutinizing the relationship between shyness and social phobia. *Journal of Anxiety Disorder*, **16**, 585–598.

Chiappa, K. H. (1983). *Evoked potentials in clinical medicine*. New York: Raven Press.

Chotai, J., & Adolfsson, R. (2002). Converging evidence suggests that monoamine neurotransmitter turnover in human adults is associated with their season of birth. *European Archives of Psychiatry and Clinical Neuroscience*, **252**, 130–134.

Chotai, J., Serretti, J., Lattuada, E., Lorenzi, C., & Lilli, R. (2003). Gene–environment interaction in psychiatric disorders as indicated by season of birth variations in tryptophan hydroxylase (TPH), serotonin transporter (5HTTLPR) and dopamine receptor (DRD4) gene polymorphisms. *Psychiatry Research*, **119**, 99–111.

Ciesla, W. (2001). Can melatonin regulate the expression of prohormone convertase 1 and 2 gene via monomeric and dimeric forms of RZR/ROR nuclear receptor, and can melatonin influence the processes of embryogenesis or carcinogenesis by disturbing the proportion of cAMP and cGMP concentrations? *Medical Hypotheses*, **56**, 181–193.

Coan, J. A., & Allen, J. J. B. (2004). Frontal EEG asymmetry as a moderator and mediator of emotion. *Biological Psychology*, **67**, 7–49.

Coplan, R. J., Rubin, K. H., Fox, N. A., Calkins, S. D., & Stuart, S. L. (1994). Being alone, playing alone, and acting alone. *Child Development*, **65**, 129–137.

Corretti, G., Pierucci, S., De Scisciolo, M., & Nisita, C. (2006). Comorbidity between social phobia and premature ejaculation: Study on 242 males affected by sexual disorders. *The Journal of Sex and Marital Therapy*, **32**, 183–187.

Cote, S., Tremblay, R. E., Nagin, D., Zoccolillo, M., & Vitaro, F. (2002). The development of impulsivity, fearfulness, and helpfulness during childhood. *Journal of Child Psychology and Psychiatry*, **43**, 609–618.

Coupland, N. J., Wilson, S. J., Potokar, J. P., Bell, C., & Nutt, D. J. (2003). Increased sympatheitc response to standing in panic disorder. *Psychiatry Research*, **118**, 69–79.

Courtet, P., Jollant, F., Buresi, C., Castelnau, D., Mouthon, D., & Malafosse, A. (2005). The monoamine oxidase A gene may influence the means used in suicide attempts. *Psychiatric Genetics*, **15**, 189–193.

Cox, B. J., MacPherson, P. S., & Enns, M. W. (2005). Psychiatric correlates of childhood shyness in a nationally representative sample. *Behavior Research and Therapy*, **43**, 1019–1027.

Craig, A. D. (2003). Interoception: The sense of the physiological condition of the body. *Current Opinion in Neurobiology*, **13**, 500–505.

Critchley, H. D. (2005). Neural mechanisms of autonomic, affective, and cognitive integration. *The Journal of Comparative Neurology*, **493**, 154–166.

Crockenberg, S. C., & Leerkes, E. M. (2005). Infant temperament moderates associations between childcare type and quantity and externalizing and internalizing behaviors at 2 1/2 years. *Infant Behavior and Development*, **28**, 20–35.

Davey, G. C., McDonald, A. S., Hirisave, U., Prabhu, G. G., Iwawaki, S., Jim, C. I., Merckelbach, H., de Jong, P. J., Leung, P. W., & Reimann, B. C. (1998). A cross-cultural study of animal fears. *Behavior Research and Therapy*, **36**, 735–750.

Davidson, R. J. (2003). Affective neuroscience and psychophysiology. *Psychophysiology*, **40**, 655–665.

Davidson, R. J., Jackson, D. L., & Kalin, N. H. (2000). Emotion, plasticity, context, and regulation. *Psychological Bulletin*, **126**, 890–909.

Davidson, S., Miller, K. A., Dowell, A., Gildea, A., & Mackenzie, A. (2006). A remote and highly conserved enhancer supports amygdala specific expression of the gene encoding the anxiogenic neuropeptide substance-P. *Molecular Psychiatry*, **11**, 410–421.

DeGrandpre, R. J., Bickel, W. K., & Higgins, S. T. (1992). Emergent equivalence relations between interoceptive (drug) and exteroceptive (visual) stimuli. *Journal of Experimental Analysis of Behavior*, **58**, 9–18.

Dekeyne, A., & Millan, M. J. (2003). Discriminative stimulus properties of antidepressant agents: A review. *Behavioral Pharmacology*, **14**, 391–407.

De Luca, A., Rizzardi, M., Buccino, A., Alessandroni, R., Salvioli, G. P., Filograsso, N., Novelli, G., & Dallapiccola, B. (2003). Association of dopamine D4 receptor (DRD4) exon III repeat polymorphism with temperament in 3-year-old infants. *Neurogenetics*, **4**, 207–212.

DiLalla, L. F., Kagan, J., & Reznick, J. S. (1994). Genetic etiology of behavioral inhibition among 2-year-old children. *Infant Behavior and Development*, **17**, 401–408.

Dillon, N. (2003). Positions, please . . .. *Nature*, **425**, 457.

Ding, Y. C., Chi, H. C., Grady, D. L., Morishima, A., Kidd, J. R., Kidd, K. K., Flodman, P., Spence, M. A., Schuck, S., Swanson, J. M., Zhang, Y. P., & Moyzis, R. K. (2002). Evidence of positive selection acting at the human dopamine receptor D4 gene locus. *Proceedings of the National Academy of Sciences*, **99**, 309–314.

Doby, V. J., & Caplan, R. D. (1995). Organizational stress as threat to reputation. *The Academy of Management Journal*, **38**, 1105–1123.

D'Souza, U. M., & Craig, I. W. (2006). Functional polymorphisms in dopamine and serotonin pathway genes. *Human Mutation*, **27**, 1–13.

REFERENCES

Eapen, V., Ghubash, R., Salem, M. O., & Sabri, S. (2005). Familial predictors of childhood shyness: A study of the United Arab Emirates population. *Community Genetics*, **8**, 61–64.

Eisenberger, N. I., Lieberman, M. D., & Satpute, A. B. (2005). Personality from a controlled processing perspective. *Cognitive, Affective, and Behavioral Neuroscience*, **5**, 169–181.

Eley, P. C., Sugden, K., Corsico, A., Gregory, A. M., Shaw, P., McGuffin, P., Plomin, R., & Craig, I. W. (2004). Gene–environment interaction analysis of serotonin system markers with adolescent depression. *Molecular Psychiatry*, **9**, 908–915.

Federmeier, K. P., & Kutas, M. (2002). Picture the difference. *Neuropsychologia*, **40**, 730–747.

Feldner, M. T., Zvolensky, M. J., Stickle, T. R., Bonn-Miller, M. O., & Leen-Feldner, E. W. (2006). Anxiety sensitivity-physical concerns as a moderator of the emotional consequences of emotion suppression during biological challenge: An experimental test using individual growth curve analysis. *Behaviour Research and Therapy*, **44**, 249–272.

Fiorilllo, C. D., Tobler, P. N., & Schultz, W. (2003). Discrete coding of reward probability and uncertainty by dopamine neurons. *Science*, **203**, 1898–2005.

Fischer, H., Andersson, J. L., Furmark, T., & Fredrikson, M. (1998). Brain correlates of an unexpected panic attack: A human positron emission topographic study. *Neuroscience Letters*, **251**, 137–140.

Fischer, P., Greitemeyer, T., Kastenmuller, A., Jonas, E., & Frey, D. (2006). Coping with terrorism. *Personality and Social Psychological Bulletin*, **32**, 365–377.

Fisher, A. B., Schaefer, B. A., Watkins, M. W., Worrell, F. C., & Hall, T. E. (2006). The factor structure of the Fear Survey Schedule for Children-II in Trinidadian children and adolescents. *Journal of Anxiety Disorders*, **20**, 740–759.

Fitzgerald, D. A., Angstadt, M., Jelsone, L. M., Nathan, P. J., & Phan, K. L. (2006). Beyond threat. *NeuroImage*, **30**, 1441–1448.

Fitzgerald, D. A., Posse, S., Moore, G. J., Tancer, M. E., Nathan, P. J., & Phan, K. L. (2004). Neural correlates of internally-generated disgust via autobiographical recall: A functional magnetic resonance imaging investigation. *Neuroscience Letters*, **11**, 91–96.

Floyd, M., Garfield, A., & LaSota, M. T. (2005). Anxiety sensitivity and worry. *Personality and Individual Differences*, **38**, 1223–1229.

Fox, N. A., Calkins, S. D., & Bell, M. A. (1994). Neural plasticity and development in the first two years of life. *Development and Psychopathology*, **6**, 677–696.

Fox, N. A., Henderson, H. A., Marshall, T. J., Nichols, K. E., & Ghera, M. N. (2005). Behavioral inhibition: Linking biology and behavior within a developmental framework. In S. T. Fiske, A. E. Kazdin & D. L. Schacter (Eds.), *Annual review of psychology* (Vol. 56, pp. 235–262). Palo Alto, CA.

Fox, N. A., Henderson, H. A., Rubin, K. H., Calkins, S. D., & Schmidt, L. A. (2001). Continuity and discontinuity of behavioral inhibition and exuberance. *Child Development*, **72**, 1–21.

Fridlund, A. J. (1994). *Human facial expression: An evolutionary view*. San Diego, CA: Academic Press Inc.

Fridlund, A. J., Hatfield, M. E., Cottam, G. L., & Fowler, S. C. (1986). Anxiety and striate muscle activation. *Journal of Abnormal Psychology*, **95**, 228–236.

Fried, I., MacDonald, K. A., & Wilson, C. L. (1997). Single neuron activity in human hippocampus and amygdala during recognition of faces and objects. *Neuron*, **18**, 753–765.

Garner, M., Mogg, K., & Bradley, B. P. (2006). Fear-relevant selective associations and social anxiety. *Behavioral Research and Therapy*, **44**, 201–217.

Goldberg, A. E., & Newlin, D. B. (2000). Season of birth and substance abuse: Findings from a large national sample. *Alcohol Clinical and Experimental Research*, **24**, 774–780.

Goldsmith, H. H., Lemery, K. S., Buss, K. A., & Campos, J. J. (1999). Genetic analyses of focal aspects of infant temperament. *Developmental Psychology*, **35**, 972–985.

Golimbet, V. E., Gritsenko, I. K., Alfimova, M. V., & Ebstein, R. P. (2005). Polymorphic markers of the dopamine D4 receptor gene promoter region and personality traits in mentally healthy individuals from the Russian population. *Genetika*, **41**, 966–972.

Gortmaker, S. L., Kagan, J., Caspi, A., & Silva, P. A. (1997). Daylength during pregnancy and shyness in children. *Developmental Psychobiology*, **31**, 107–114.

Gould, R. V. (2003). *Collision of Wills*. Chicago: Il. University of Chicago Press.

Grabe, H. J., Lange, M., Wolff, B., Volzke, H., Lucht, M., Freyberger, H. J., John, U., & Cascorbi, I. (2005). Mental and physical distress is modulated in the 5-HT transporter gene interacting with social stressors and chronic disease burden. *Molecular Psychiatry*, **10**, 220–224.

Grinband, J., Hirsch, J., & Ferrera, V. P. (2006). A neural representation of categorization uncertainty in the human brain. *Neuron*, **49**, 757–763.

Hacking, I. (1990). *The taming of chance*. New York: Cambridge University Press.

Hagemann, D., Hewig, J., Seifert, J., Naumann, E., & Bartussek, D. (2005). The latent state–trait structure of resting EEG asymmetry. *Psychophysiology*, **42**, 740–752.

Hagemann, D., Naumann, E., Thayer, J. F., & Bartussek, D. (2002). Does resting EEG asymmetry reflect a trait? *Journal of Personality and Social Psychology*, **82**, 619–641.

Hallowell, A. I. (1941). The social function of anxiety in a primitive society. *American Sociological Review*, **6**, 869–891.

Handa, R. J., Nunley, K. M., Lorens, S. A., Louie, J. P., McGivern, R. F., & Bullnow, M. R. (1994). Androgen regulation of adrenocorticotropin and corticosterone secretion in the male rat following novelty and foot shock stressors. *Physiology and Behavior*, **55**, 117–124.

Hanson, D. K., Jones, B. A., & Watson, N. V. (2004). Distribution of androgen receptor immunoreactivity in the brainstem of male rats. *Neuroscience*, **127**, 797–803.

Hare, E. H. (1975). Manic-depressive psychosis and season of birth. *Acta Psychiatrica Scandinavia*, **52**, 69–79.

Hariri, A. R., & Brown, S. M. (2006). Serotonin. *The American Journal of Psychiatry*, **163**, 12.

Hariri, A. R., Drabant, E. M., & Weinberger, D. R. (2006). Imaging genetics: Perspectives from studies of genetically driven variation in serotonin function and corticolimbic affective processing. *Biological Psychiatry*, **59**, 888–897.

Hartl, D., & Jones, E. W. (2005). *Genetics* (6th ed.). Boston: Jones & Bartlett.

Heinrichs, N., Rapee, R. M., Alden, L. A., Bogels, S., Hoffmann, S. G., Ja Oh, K., & Sakano, Y. (2006). Cultural differences in perceived social norms and social anxiety. *Behaviour Research and Therapy*, **44**, 1187–1197.

Hendricks-Ferguson, V. (2006). Relationships of age and gender to hope and spiritual well-being among adolescents with cancer. *Journal of Oncological Nursing*, **23**, 189–199.

Herman, A. I., Kaiss, K. M., Ma, R., Philbeck, J. W., Hasan, A., Dasti, H., & DePetrillo, P. B. (2005). Serotonin transporter promoter polymorphism and monoamine oxidase type A VNTR allelic variants together influence alcohol binge drinking risk in young women. *American Journal of Medical Genetics B Neuropsychiatric Genetics*, **133**, 74–78.

Hinton, D. E., Pich, V., Chhean, D., Pollack, M. H., & McNally, R. J. (2005b). Sleep paralysis among Cambodian refugees: Association with PTSD diagnosis and severity. *Depression and Anxiety*, **22**, 47–51.

Hinton, D. E., Pich, V., Safren, S. A., Pollack, M. H., & McNally, R. J. (2005a). Anxiety sensitivity in traumatized Cambodian refugees. *Behavioral Research and Therapy*, **43**, 1631–1643.

Hoehn-Saric, R., Hazlett, R. L., Pourmotabbed, T., & McLeod, D. R. (1997). Does muscle tension reflect arousal? *Psychiatry Research*, **16**, 49–51.

Hoehn-Saric, R., Lee, J. S., McLeod, D. R., & Wong, D. F. (2005). Effect of worry on regional cerebral blood flow in nonanxious subjects. *Psychiatry Research: Neuroimaging*, **140**, 259–269.

Hofmann, S. G., Moscovitch, D. A., Litz, B. T., Kim, H. J., Davis, L. L., & Pizzagalli, D. A. (2005). The worried mind: Autonomic and prefrontal activation during worrying. *Emotion*, **5**, 464–475.

Holland, P. C., & Gallagher, M. (2004). Amygdala–frontal interactions and reward expectancy. *Current Opinion in Neurobiology*, **14**, 148–155.

Holmes, A., Winston, J. S., & Eimer, M. (2005). The role of spatial frequency information for ERP components sensitive to faces and emotional facial expression. *Cognitive Brain Research*, **25**, 508–520.

Hsu, M., Bhatt, M., Adolphus, R., Tranel, D., & Camerer, C. F. (2005). Neural systems responding to degrees of uncertainty in human decision-making. *Science*, **310**, 1680–1683.

Huber, D., Veinante, P., & Stoop, R. (2005). Vasopressin and oxytocin excite distinct neuronal populations in the central amygdala. *Science*, **308**, 245–248.

Hughes, A. A., Heimberg, R. G., Coles, M. E., Gibb, B. E., Liebowitz, M. R., & Schneier, F. R. (2006). Relations of the factors of the tripartite model of anxiety and depression to types of social anxiety. *Behaviour Research and Therapy*, **44**, 1629–1641.

Husted, D. S., Shapira, N. A., & Goodman, W. K. (2006). The neurocircuitry of obsessive–compulsive disorder and disgust. *Progress in neuropsychopharmacology and Biological Psychiatry*, **30**, 389–399.

Hyde, J. S. (2005). The gender similarities hypothesis. *American Psychologist*, **60**, 581–592.

Irizarry, Y., & Galbraith, S. J. (2004). Complex disorders reloaded: Causality, action, reaction, cause and effect. *Molecular Psychiatry*, **9**, 431–432.

Izquierdo, I. (1987). The effect of an exposure to novel and non-novel video taped material on retrieval in two memory tests. *Neuropsychologia*, **25**, 995–998.

Izquierdo, L. A., Barros, D. M., Medina, J. H., & Izquierdo, I. (2003). Exposure to novelty enhances retrieval of very remote memory in rats. *Neurobiology of Learning and Memory*, **79**, 51–56.

Johanson, A., Gustafson, L., Passant, U., Risberg, J., Smith, G., Warkentin, S., & Tucker, D. (1998). Brain function in spider phobia. *Psychiatry Research Neuroimaging*, **84**, 101–111.

Joiner, T. E., Pfaff, J. J., Acres, J. G., & Johnson, F. (2002). Birth month and suicidal and depressive symptoms in Australians born in the Southern vs. the Northern Hemisphere. *Psychiatry Research*, **112**, 89–92.

Jones, B. C., Hou, X., & Cook, M. N. (1996). Effect of exposure to novelty on brain monoamines in C57BL/6 and DBA/2 mice. *Physiology and Behavior*, **59**, 361–367.

Jung, J., Hudry, J., Ryvlin, P., Royet, J., Bertrand, O., & Lachaux, J. (2005). Functional significance of olfactory-induced oscillations in the human amygdala. *Cerebral Cortex*, **16**, 1–8.

Kagan, J. (1994). *Galen's prophecy*. New York: Basic Books.

Kagan, J., Arcus, D., Snidman, N., Feng, W. U., Hendler, J., & Greene, S. (1994). Reactivity in infants: A cross-national comparison. *Developmental Psychology*, **30**, 342–345.

Kagan, J., Reznick, J. S., & Snidman, N. (1988). Biological bases of childhood shyness. *Science*, **240**, 167–171.

Kagan, J., & Saudino, K. J. (2001). Behavioral inhibition and related temperaments. In R. N. Emde & J. K. Hewitt (Eds.), *Infants early childhood* (pp. 111–122). New York: Oxford University Press.

Kagan, J., & Snidman, N. (2004). *The long shadow of temperament*. Cambridge, MA: Harvard University Press.

Kagan, J., Snidman, N., & Arcus, D. (1998). Childhood derivatives of high- and low-reactivity in infancy. *Child Development*, **69**, 1483–1493.

Kanbara, K., Mitani, Y., Fukunaga, M., Ishino, S., Takebayashi, N., & Nakai, Y. (2004). Paradoxical results of psychophysiological stress profiles in functional somatic syndrome. *Applied Psychophysiology and Biofeedback*, **29**, 255–268.

Kandel, E. R. (1983). From metapsychology to molecular biology. *The American Journal of Psychiatry*, **40**, 1277–1293.

Kandiel, A., Chen, S., & Hillman, D. E. (1999). c-fos gene expression parallels auditory adaptation in the adult rat. *Brain Research*, **839**, 292–297.

Kashdan, T. B., Julian, T., Merritt, K., & Uswatte, G. (2006). Social anxiety and posttraumatic stress in combat veterans: Relation to well-being and character strengths. *Behaviour Reseach and Therapy*, **44**, 561–583.

Kashdan, T. B., & Steger, M. F. (2006). Expanding the topography of social anxiety. *Psychological Science*, **17**, 120–128.

Kaufman, J., Yang, B. Z., Douglas-Palumberi, H., Houssyar, S., Lipschitz, D., Krystal, J. H., & Gelertner, J. (2004). Social supports and serotonin transporter gene modulate depression in maltreated children. *Proceedings of the National Academy of Sciences*, **101**, 17316–17321.

Kelly, M. M., Forsyth, J. P., & Karekla, M. (2006). Sex differences in response to a panicogenic challenge procedure: An experimental evaluation of panic vulnerability in a non-clinical sample. *Behaviour Research and Therapy*, **44**, 1421–1430.

Kelly, O. P., McIntosh, J., McIntyre, D. C., Merali, Z., & Anisman, H. (2003). Anxiety in rats selectively bred for fast and slow kindling rates: Situation-specific outcomes. *Stress*, **6**, 289–295.

Kent, J. M., Coplan, J. D., Mawlawi, O., Martinez, J. M., Browne, S. T., Slifstein, M., Martinez, D., Abi-Dargham, A., Laruelle, M., & Gorman, J. M. (2005). Prediction of panic response to a respiratory stimulant by reduced orbitofrontal cerebral blood flow in panic disorder. *American Journal of Psychiatry*, **162**, 1379–1381.

Kerr, J. E., Beck, S. G., & Handa, R. J. (1996). Androgens selectively modulate C-fos messenger RNA induction in the rat hippocampus following novelty. *Neuroscience*, **74**, 757–766.

Kerr, M., Lambert, W. W., & Bem, D. J. (1996). Life course sequelae of childhood shyness in Sweden: Comparison with the United States. *Developmental Psychology*, **32**, 1100–1105.

Kessler, R. C., Berglund, P., Demler, O., Jin, R., & Walters, E. E. 2005. Lifetime prevalence and age-of-onset distribution of DSM-IV disorders in the National Cormobidity Survey replication. *Archives of General Psychiatry*, **62**, 593–602.

Kim, H., Somerville, L. H., Johnstone, T., Polis, S., Alexander, A. L., Shin, L. M., & Whalen, P. J. (2004). Contextual modulation of amygdala responsivity to surprised faces. *Journal of Cognitive Neuroscience*, **16**, 1730–1745.

Kirsch, P., Esslinger, C., Chen, Q., Mier, D., Lis, S., Siddhanti, S., Gruppe, H., Mattay, V. S., Gallhofer, B., & Meyer-Lindenberg, A. (2005). Oxytocin modulates neural circuitry for social cognition and fear to humans. *Journal of Neuroscience*, **49**, 11489–11493.

Kitchigina, V., Vankov, A., Harley, C., & Sara, S. J. (1997). Novelty elicited, noradrenaline-dependent enhancement of excitability in the dentate gyrus. *The European Journal of Neuroscience*, **9**, 41–47.

Koh, M. T., Wilkins, E. E., & Bernstein, I. L. (2003). Novel tastes elevate c-fos expression in the central amygdala and insular cortex: Implication for taste aversion learning. *Behavioral Neuroscience*, **117**, 1416–1422.

Kotler, M., Cohen, H., Segman, R., Gritsenko, I., Nemanov, L., Lerer, B., Kramer, I., Zer-Zion, M., Kletz, I., & Ebstein, R. P. (1997). Excess dopamine D4 receptor (D4DR) Exon III 7 repeat allele in opioid-dependent subjects. *Molecular Psychiatry*, **2**, 251–254.

Kuraoka, K., & Nakamura, K. (2006). Impacts of facial identity and type of emotion on responses of amygdalar neurons. *Neuroreport*, **17**, 9–12.

La Gasse, L., Gruber, C., & Lipsitt, L. P. (1989). The infantile expression of avidity in relation to later assessments. In J. S. Reznick (Ed.), *Perspectives on behavioral inhibition* (pp. 159–176). Chicago, IL: University of Chicago Press.

Lahti, J., Raikkonen, K., Ekelund, J., Peltonen, L., Raitakari, O. T., & Keltikangas-Jarvinen, L. (2006). Socio-demographic characteristics moderate the association between DRD4 and novelty seeking. *Personality and Individual Differences*, **40**, 533–543.

Lakatos, K., Nemoda, Z., Birkas, E., Ronai, Z., Kovacs, E., Ney, K., Toth, I., Sasvari-Szekely, M., & Gervai, J. (2003). Association of D4 dopamine receptor gene and serotonin transporter promoter polymorphism with infants' response to novelty. *Molecular Psychiatry*, **8**, 90–98.

Laugesen, N., Dugas, M. J., & Bukowski, W. M. (2003). Understanding adolescent worry: The application of a cognitive model. *Journal of Abnormal Child Psychology*, **31**, 55–64.

Leech, S. L., Larkby, C. A., Day, R., & Day, N. L. (2006). Predictors and correlates of high levels of depression and anxiety symptoms among children at age 10. *Journal of the American Academy of Child and Adolescent Psychiatry*, **45**, 223–230.

Liddell, B. J., Brown, K. J., Kemp, A. H., Barton, J. J., Das, P., Peduto, A., Gordon, E., & Williams, L. M. (2005). A direct brainsteam–amygdala–cortical 'alarm' for subliminal signals of fear. *NeuroImage*, **24**, 235–243.

Loewy, A. D. (1990). Anatomy of the autonomic nervous system. In A. D. Loewy & K. M. Spyer (Eds.), *Central regulation of autonomic functions* (pp. 3–16). New York: Oxford University Press.

Manuck, S. B., Flory, J. D., Ferrell, R. E., & Muldoon, M. F. (2004). Socio-economic status covaries with central nervous system serotonergic responsivity as a function of allelic variation in the serotonin transporter gene-linked polymorphic region. *Psychoneuroendocrinology*, **29**, 651–668.

Marsh, R. H., Fuzessery, Z. M., Grose, C. D., & Wenstrupp, J. J. 2002. Projection to the inferior colliculus from the basal nucleus of the amygdala. *Journal of Neuroscience*, **22**, 10449–10460.

Marshall, P. J., & Fox, N. A. (2005). Relations between behavioral reactivity at 4 months and attachment classification at 14 months in a selected sample. *Infant Behavior and Development*, **28**, 495–502.

Masia-Warner, C., Klein, R. G., Dent, H. C., Fisher, P. H., Alvir, J., Albano, A. M., & Guardino, M. (2005). School-based intervention for adolescents with social anxiety disorder: Results of a controlled study. *Journal of Abnormal Child Psychology*, **33**, 707–722.

Masten, A. S., Burk, K. B., Roisman, G. I., Obradovic, J., Long, J. D., & Tellegen, A. (2004). Resources and resilience in the transition to adulthood: Continuity and change. *Development and Psychopathology*, **16**, 1071–1094.

Matheny, A. (1990). Developmental behavior gentetics. In M. E. Hahn, J. K. Hewitt, N. D. Henderson & R. H. Benno (Eds.), *Developmental behavioral genetics* (pp. 25–38). New York: Oxford University Press.

McDonald, A. J. (2003). Is there an amygdala and how far does it extend? An anatomical perspective. *Annals of the New York Academy of Sciences*, **985**, 1–21.

McLin, P. E., Miasnikov, A. A., & Weinberger, N. M. (2002). The effect of electrical stimulation of the nucleus basalis on the electroencephalogram, heart rate, and respiration. *Behavioral Neuroscience*, **116**, 795–806.

Meller, S. T., & Dennis, B. J. (1991). Efferent projections of the periaqueductal gray in the rabbit. *Neuroscience*, **40**, 191–216.

Merali, Z., McIntosh, J., Kent, T., Michaud, D., & Anisman, H. (1998). Aversive and appetitive events evoke the release of corticotropin-releasing hormone and

Bombesin-like peptides of the central nucleus of the amygdala. *Journal of Neuroscience*, **18**, 4758–4766.

Merikangas, K. R., Lieb, R., Wittchen, H. U., & Avenevoli, S. (2003). Family and high-risk studies of social anxiety disorder. *Acta Psychiatrica Scandinavia*, **417** (Suppl.), 28–37.

Mineka, S., & Zinbarg, R. (2006). A contemporary learning theory perspective on the etiology of anxiety disorder. *American Psychologist*, **61**, 10–26.

Minoshima, I., & Okagami, K. (2000). Seasonality of birth in patients with mood disorders in Japan. *Journal of Affective Disorders*, **59**, 41–46.

Mohapel, P., & McIntyre, D. C. (1998). Amygdala kindling-resistant (SLOW) or prone (FAST) rat strains showed differential fear responses. *Behavioral Neuroscience*, **112**, 1402–1413.

Mohr, C., Binkofski, F., Erdmann, C., Buchel, C., & Helmchen, C. (2005). The anterior cingulate cortex contains distinct areas dissociating external from self-administered painful stimulation: A parametric fMRI study. *Pain*, **114**, 347–357.

Momozawa, Y., Takeuchi, Y., Kusunose, R., Kikusui, T., & Mori, Y. 2005. Association between equine temperament and polymorphisms in dopamine D4 receptor genes. *Mammalian Genome*, **16**, 538–544.

Moncada, D., & Viola, H. (2006). Phosphorylation state of CREB in the rat hippocampus: A molecular switch between spatial novelty and spatial familiarity? *Neurobiology of Learning and Memory* (in press).

Moriguchi, Y., Ohnishi, T., Kawachi, T., Mori, T., Hirakata, M., Yamada, M., Matsuda, H., & Komaki, G. (2005). Specific brain activation in Japanese and Caucasian people to fearful faces. *Neuroreport*, **16**, 133–136.

Morley-Fletcher, S., Polanza, P., Parolaro, D., Vigaro, D., & Laviola, G. (2003). Intra-uterine position has long term influences on brain mu-opioid receptor densities and behavior in mice. *Psychoneuroendicrinology*, **28**, 386–400.

Morrison, I., Lloyd, D., Di Pellegrino, G., & Roberts, N. (2004). Vicarious responses to pain in anterior cingulate cortex: Is empathy a multisensory issue? *Cognitive, Affective, and Behavioral Neuroscience*, **4**, 270–278.

Naatanen, R., & Pickton, T. (1997). The N1 wave of the human electric and magnetic response to sound. *Psychophysiology*, **24**, 375–425.

Netter, P. (2006). Dopamine challenge tests as an indicator of psychological traits. *Human Psychopharmacology* (in press).

Nilsson, K. W., Sjoberg, R. L., Dambey, M., Leppert, J., Ohrvik, J., Alm, P. O., Lindstrom, L., & Oreland, L. (2005). Role of monoamine oxidase A genotype and psychosocial factors in male adolescent criminal activity. *Biological Psychiatry*, **59**, 121–127.

O'Kane, J., Insler, R. Z., & Wagner, A. D. (2005). Conceptual and perceptual novelty effects in human medial temporal cortex. *Hippocampus*, **15**, 326–332.

Olino, T. M., Klein, D. N., Durbin, C. E., Hayden, E. P., & Buckley, M. E. (2005). The structure of extraversion in preschool aged children. *Personality and Individual Differences*, **39**, 481–492.

Onaka, T., & Yagi, K. (1993). Effects of novelty stress on vasopressin and oxytocin secretion by the pituitary in the rat. *Journal of Neuroendicrinology*, **5**, 365–369.

Ono, S., & Nishijo, H. (2000). Neurophysiological bases of emotion in primates. In M. Gazzaniga (Ed.), *New cognitive neuroscience* (2nd ed., pp. 1099–1114). Cambridge, MA: MIT Press.

Oya, H., Kawasaki, H., Howard, M. A. III, & Adolphs, R. (2002). Electrophysiological responses in the human amygdala discriminate emotion categories of complex visual stimuli. *Journal of Neuroscience*, **22**, 9502–9512.

Pape, H. C., & Stork, O. (2003). Genes and mechanisms in the amygdala involved in the formation of fear memory. *Annals of the New York Academy of Sciences*, **985**, 92–105.

Parr, L. A., Waller, B. M., & Fugate, J. (2005). Emotional communication in primates: Implications for neurobiology. *Current Opinion in Neurobiology*, **15**, 716–720.

Parsey, R. V., Hastings, R. S., Oquendo, M. A., Hu, X., Goldman, D., Huang, Y., Simpson, N., Arcement, J., Huang, Y., Ogden, T., Van Heertum, R. L., Arango, V., & Mann, J. J. (2006a). Effect of a triallelic functional polymorphism of the serotonin-transporter-linked promoter region on expression of serotonin transporter in the human brain. *American Journal of Psychiatry*, **163**, 48–51.

Parsey, R. V., Hastings, R. S., Oquendo, M. A., Huang, Y. Y., Simpson, N., Arcement, J., Huang, Y., Ogden, R. T., Van Heertum, R. L., Arango, V., & Mann, J. J. (2006b). Lower serotonin transporter binding potential in the human brain during major depressive episodes. *American Journal of Psychiatry*, **163**, 52–58.

Paton, J. J., Belova, M. A., Morrison, S. E., & Salzman, C. D. (2006). The primate amygdala represents the positive and negative value of visual stimuli during learning. *Nature*, **439**, 865–870.

Pauli, P., Wiedemann, G., & Nickola, M. (1999). Pain sensitivity, cerebral laterality, and negative affect. *Pain*, **80**, 359–364.

Perez-Gonzalez, D., Malmierca, M. S., & Covey, E. (2005). Novelty disorder neurons in the mammalian auditory midbrain. *European Journal of Neuroscience*, **22**, 2879–2885.

Petrovich, G. D., Centeras, N. S., & Swanson, L. W. (2001). Combinatorial amygdalar inputs to hippocampal and hypothalamic behavioral systems. *Brain Research Reviews*, **38**, 247–289.

Pfister, H. P., & Muir, J. L. (1989). Influence of exogenously administered oxytocin on central noradrenaline dopamine and serotonin levels following psychological stress in nulliparous female rats (*Rattus norvegicus*). *International Journal of Neuroscience*, **45**, 221–229.

Phelps, E. A. (2006). Emotion and cognition. In S. T. Fiske, A. E. Kazdin & D. L. Schacter (Eds.), *Annual review of psychology* (Vol. 57, pp. 27–53). Palo Alto, CA.

Pitkanen, A. (2000). Connectivity of the rat amygdaloid complex. In J. P. Aggleton (Ed.), *The amygdala* (2nd ed.). New York: Oxford University Press.

Pjrek, E., Winkler, D., Heiden, A., Praschak-Rieder, N., Willeit, M., Konstantinidis, A., Stastny, J., & Kasper, S. (2004). Seasonality of birth in seasonal affective disorder. *Journal of Clinical Psychiatry*, **65**, 1389–1393.

Pollatos, O., Kirsch, W., & Schandry, R. (2005). Brain structures involved in interoceptive awareness and cardioafferent signal processing. *Human Brain Mapping*, **26**, 54–64.

Posthuma, D., DeGeus, E. J. C., Mulder, E. J. C. M., Smit, D. J. A., Boomsma, D. I., & Stam, C. J. (2005). Genetic components of functional connectivity in the brain. *Human Brain Mapping*, **26**, 191–198.

Potts, G. F., Patel, S. H., & Azzam, P. N. (2004). The impact of instrumental relevance on the visual ERP. *International Journal of Psychophysiology*, **52**, 197–209.

Price, J. L. (2005). Free will versus survival. *Journal of Comparative Neurology*, **493**, 132–139.

Prior, M., Smart, D., Sanson, A., & Oberklaid, F. (2000). Does shy-inhibited temperament in childhood lead to anxiety problems in adolescence? *Journal of the American Academy of Child and Adolescent Psychiatry*, **39**, 461–468.

Rankin, C. H. (2000). Context conditioning in habituation in the nematode Caenorhabiditis elegans. *Behavioral Neuroscience*, **114**, 496–505.

Ray, J., Hansen, S., & Waters, N. (2006). Links between temperamental dimensions and brain monoamines in the rat. *Behavioral Neuroscience*, **120**, 85–92.

Reinscheid, R. K., & Xu, Y. L. (2005). Neuropeptide S as a novel arousal promoting peptide transmitter. *European Journal of Biochemistry*, **272**, 5689–5693.

Reuter, M., & Hennig, J. (2005). Association of the functional catechol-o-methyltransferase VAL158MET polymorphism with the personality trait of extraversion. *Neuroreport*, **16**, 1135–1138.

Riggio, H. R., & Riggio, R. E. (2002). Emotional expressiveness, extraversion, and neuroticism: A meta-analysis. *Journal of Nonverbal Behavior*, **26**, 195–218.

Rinberg, D., & Davidowitz, H. (2000). Do cockroaches know about fluid dynamics? *Nature*, **405**, 756.

Rollnik, J. D., Schmitz, N., & Kugler, J. (2001). Cardiovascular reactions induced by unpredictable, predictable, and controllable painful stimuli during sphygmomanometry. *International Journal of Psychophysiology*, **40**, 161–165.

Rolls, E. T., Browning, A. S., Inoue, K., & Hernadi, I. (2005). Novel visual stimuli activate a population of neurons in the primate orbitofrontal cortex. *Neurobiology of Learning and Memory*, **84**, 111–123.

Roney, J. R., & Maestripieri, D. (2004). Relative digit lengths predict men's behavior and attractiveness during social interaction with women. *Human Nature*, **15**, 271–282.

Rosen, J. B., Adamec, R. E., & Thompson, B. L. (2005). Expression of egr-1 (zif268) mRNA in select fear-related brain regions following exposure to a predator. *Behavioral Brain Research*, **162**, 279–288.

Rosenbaum, J. F., Biederman, J., Hirshfeld, D. R., Bolduc, E. A., Faraone, S. V., Kagan, J., Snidman, N., & Reznick, J. S. (1991). Further evidence of an association between behavioral inhibition and anxiety disorders: Results from a family study of children from a non-clinical sample. *Journal of Psychiatric Research*, **25**, 49–65.

Rothbart, M. K. (1989). Temperament in childhood. In J. A. Kohnstamm, J. E. Bates & M. K. Rothbart (Eds.), *Temperament in childhood* (pp. 59–76). New York: Wiley.

Rozin, P., & Cohen, A. B. (2003). High frequency of facial expression corresponding to confusion, concentration, and worry in an analysis of naturally occurring facial expressions of Americans. *Emotion*, **3**, 68–75.

Rubin, K. H., Burgess, K. B., & Hastings, D. D. (2002). The stability and social behavioral consequences of toddler's inhibited temperament and parenting behaviors. *Child Development*, **73**, 483–495.

Rybak, M., Crayton, J. W., Young, I. J., Herba, E., & Konopka, L. M. (2006). Frontal alpha power asymmetry in aggressive children and adolescents with mood and disruptive behavior disorders. *Clinical EEG and Neuroscience*, **37**, 16–24.

Samochowiec, J., Hajduk, A., Samochowiec, A., Horodnicki, J., Stepie, G., Grzywacz, A., & Kucharska-Mazur, J. (2004). Association studies of MAO-A, COMT, and 5-HTT genes polymorphisms in patients with anxiety disorders of the phobic spectrum. *Psychiatry Research*, **128**, 21–26.

Sanders, G., Bereczkei, T., Csatho, A., & Manning, J. 2005. The ratio of the 2nd to the 4th finger length predicts spatial ability in men but not women. *Cerebral Cortex*, **41**, 789–792.

Sara, S. J., Dyon-Laurent, C., & Herve, A. (1995). Novelty-seeking behavior in the rat is dependent upon the integrity of the noradrenergic system. *Brain Research Cognitive Brain Research*, **2**, 181–187.

Schafer, A., Schienle, A., & Vaitl, D. (2005). Stimulus type and design influence hemodynamic responses towards visual disgust and fear elicitors. *International Journal of Psychophysiology*, **57**, 53–59.

Schienle, A., Schafer, A., Hermann, A., Walter, B., Stark, R., & Vaitl, D. (2006). fMRI responses to pictures of mutilation and contamination. *Neuroscience Letters*, **393**, 174–178.

Schmidt, L. A., Fox, N. A., Schulkin, J., & Gold, P. W. (1999). Behavioral and psychophysiological correlates of self-presentation in temperamentally shy children. *Developmental Psychobiology*, **35**, 119–135.

Schmidt, L. A., Trainor, L. J., & Santesso, D. L. (2003). Developmental of frontal electroencephalogram (EEG) and heart rate (ECG) responses to affective musical stimuli during the first 12 months of postnatal life. *Brain and Cognition*, **52**, 27–32.

Schmutz, S. M., & Schmutz, J. K. (1998). Heritability estimates of behaviors associated with hunting in dogs. *Journal of Heredity*, **89**, 233–237.

Schneirla, T. C. (1959). An evolutionary and developmental theory of biphasic processes approach and withdrawal. In M. R. Jones (Ed.), *Nebraska symposium on motivation* (pp. 1–44). Lincoln: University of Nebraska Press.

Schultz, W. (2006). Reward and addiction. In S. T. Fiske, A. E. Kazdin & D. L. Schacter (Eds.), *Annual review of psychology* (Vol. 57, pp. 87–116). Palo Alto, CA.

Schulz, G. M., Varga, N., Jeffires, K., Ludlow, C. L., & Braun, A. R. (2005). Functional neuroanatomy of human vocalization. *Cerebral Cortex*, **15**, 1835–1847.

Schwartz, C. E., Wright, C. I., Shin, L. M., Kagan, J., & Rauch, S. L. (2003). Inhibited and uninhibited infants grown up. *Science*, **300**, 1952–1953.

Scott, J. P., & Fuller, J. (1965). *Genetics and the social behavior of the dog*. Chicago, IL: University of Chicago Press.

Servatius, R. J., & Beck, K. D. (2005). Mild interoceptive stressors affect learning and reactivity to contextual cues: Toward understanding the development of unexplained illnesses. *Neuropsychopharmacology*, **30**, 1483–1491.

Simm, R. W., & Nath, L. E. (2004). Gender and emotion. *American Journal of Sociology*, **109**, 1137–1176.

Sivan, Y., Laudon, M., Tauman, R., & Zisapel, N. (2001). Melatonin production in healthy infants: Evidence for seasonal variations. *Pediatric Research*, **49**, 63–68.

Smit, A. S., Eling, P. A. T. M., & Coenen, A. M. L. (2004). Mental effort affects vigilance enduringly: After-effects in EEG and behavior. *International Journal of Psychophysiology*, **53**, 239–243.

Smit, D. J. A., Posthuma, D., Boomsma, D. I., & DeGues, E. J. C. (2005). Heritability of background EEG across the power spectrum. *Psychophysiology*, **42**, 691–697.

Smoller, J. W., Yamaki, L. H., Fagerness, J. A., Biederman, J., Racette, S., Laird, N. M., Kagan, J., Snidman, N., Faraone, S. V., Hirshfeld-Becker, D., Tsuang, M. T., Slaugenhaupt, S. A., Rosenbaum, J. F., & Sklar, P. B. (2005). The corticotropin-releasing hormone gene and behavioral inhibition in children at risk for panic disorder. *Biological Psychiatry*, **15**, 1485–1492.

Stabell, K. E., Andresen, S., Bakke, S. J., Bjornaes, H., Borchgrevink, H. M., Heminghyt, E., & Roste, G. K. (2004). Emotional responses during unilateral amobarbital anesthesia: Differential hemispheric contributions. *Acta Neurologica Scandinavia*, **110**, 313–321.

Stark, R., Schienle, A., Girod, C., Walter, B., Kirsch, P., Blecker, C., Ott, U., Schafer, A., Sammer, G., Zimmerman, M., & Vital, D. (2005). Erotic and disgust inducing pictures—differences in the hemodynamic responses of the brain. *Biological Psychology*, **70**, 19–29.

Stark, R., Schienle, A., Walter, B., Kirsch, P., Sammer, G., Ott, U., Blecker, C., & Vaitl, D. (2003). Hemodynamic responses to fear and disgust-inducing pictures: An fMRI study. *International Journal of Psychophysiology*, **50**, 225–234.

Stefanacci, L., & Amaral, D. G. (2002). Some observations on cortical input for the macaque amygdala. *Journal of Comparative Neurology*, **451**, 301–323.

Stein, M. B., Fallin, M. D., Schork, N. J., & Gelernter, J. (2005). COMT polymorphisms and anxiety-related personality traits. *Neuropsychopharmacology*, **30**, 2092–2102.

Stein, M. B., Jang, K. L., & Livesley, W. J. (1999). Heritability of anxiety sensitivity: A twin study. *American Journal of Psychiatry*, **156**, 246–251.

Strange, B. A., Hurlemann, R., Duggins, A., Heinz, H. J., & Dolan, R. J. (2005). Dissociating intentional learning from relative novelty responses in the medial temporal lobe. *NeuroImage*, **25**, 51–62.

Sundet, J. M., Skre, I., Okkenhaug, J. J., & Tambs, K. (2003). Genetic and environmental causes of the interrelationships between self-reported fears. A study of a non-clinical sample of Norwegian identical twins and their families. *Scandinavian Journal of Psychology*, **44**, 97–106.

Surtees, P. G., Wainwright, N. W. J., Willis-Owen, S. A. G., Luben, R., Day, N. E., & Flint, J. (2006). Social adversity, the serotonin transporter (5-HTTLPR) polymorphism and major depressive disorder. *Biological Psychiatry*, **59**, 224–229.

Sutton, S. K., Burnette, C. P., Mundy, P. C., Meyer, J., Vaughan, A., Sanders, C., & Yale, M. (2005). Resting cortical brain activity and social behavior in higher functioning children with autism. *Journal of Child Psychology and Psychiatry*, **46**, 211–222.

Sutton, S. K., & Davidson, R. J. (2000). Prefrontal brain electrical asymmetry predicts the evaluation of affective stimuli. *Neuropsychologia*, **38**, 723–733.

Szekely, A., Ronai, Z., Nemoda, Z., Kolmann, G., Gervai, J., & Sasvari-Szekely, M. (2004). Human personality dimensions of persistence and harm avoidance associated with DRD4 and 5-HTTLPR polymorphisms. *American Journal of Medical Genetics: Neuropsychiatric Genetics*, **126**, 106–110.

Thomas, L., Purvis, C. C., Drew, J. E., Abramovich, D. R., & Williams, L. M. (2002). Melatonin receptors in human fetal brain: 2-[(125)I] indomelatonin binding and MT1 gene expression. *The Journal of Pineal Research*, **33**, 218–224.

Timonen, M., Jokelainen, J., Hakko, H., Silvennoinen-Kassinen, S., Meyer-Rochow, V. B., Herva, A., & Rasanen, P. (2003). Atopy and depression: Results from the Northern Finland 1996 Birth Cohort Study. *Molecular Psychiatry*, **8**, 738–744.

Tops, M., Wijers, A. A., van Staveren, A. S., Bruin, K. J., Den Boer, J. A., Meijman, T. F., & Korf, J. (2005). Acute cortisol administration modulates EEG alpha asymmetry in volunteers: Relevance to depression. *Biological Psychology*, **69**, 181–193.

Torres-Farton, C., Richter, H. G., Germain, A. M., Valenzuela, G. J., Campino, C., Rojas-Garcia, P., Forcelledo, M. L., Torrealba, F., & Seron-Ferre, M. (2004). Maternal melatonin selectively inhibits cortisol production in the primate fetal adrenal gland. *The Journal of Physiology*, **554**, 841–856.

Torrey, E. F., Miller, J., Rawlings, R., & Yolken, R. H. (1997). Seasonality of births in schizophrenia and bipolar disorder: A review of the literature. *Schizophrenia Research*, **28**, 1–38.

van Anders, S. M., Vernon, P. A., & Wilbur, C. J. (2006). Finger-length ratios show evidence of prenatal hormone-transfer between opposite-sex twins. *Hormones and Behavior*, **49**, 315–319.

Vuga, M., Fox, N. A., Cohn, F., George, C. J., Levensein, R. M., & Kovacs, M. (2006). Long-term stability of frontal electroencephalographic asymmetry in adults with a history of depression and controls. *International Journal of Psychophysiology*, **59**, 107–115.

Waller, B. M., & Dunbar, R. I. M. (2005). Differential behavioural effects of silent bared teeth display and relaxed open mouth display in chimpanzees (*Pan troglodytes*). *Ethology*, **111**, 129–143.

Wassermann, E. M., Greenberg, B. D., Nguyen, M. B., & Murphy, D. L. (2001). Motor cortex excitability correlates with an anxiety-related personality trait. *Biological Psychiatry*, **50**, 377–382.

Weich, S., Twigg, L., & Lewis, G. (2006). Rural/non-rural differences in rates of common mental disorders in Britain. *The British Journal of Psychiatry*, **188**, 51–57.

Wiedemann, G., Pauli, P., Dengler, W., Lutzenberger, W., Birbaumer, N., & Buchkremer, G. (1999). Frontal brain asymmetry as a biological substrate of emotions in patients with panic disorders. *Archives of General Psychiatry*, **56**, 78–84.

Williams, L. M., Barton, M. J., Kemp, A. H., Liddell, P. J., Peduto, A., Gordon, E., & Bryant, R. A. (2005). Distinct amygdala-autonomic arousal profiles in response to fear signals in healthy males and females. *NeuroImage*, **28**, 618–626.

Willinger, U., & Aschauer, H. N. (2005). Personality, anxiety and functional dysphonia. *Personality and Individual Differences*, **39**, 1441–1449.

Wirtschafter, D. (2005). Cholinergic involvement in the cortical and hippocampal c-Fos expression induced in the rat by placement in a novel environment. *Brain Research*, **1051**, 57–65.

Witter, M. P., Wouterlood, F. G., Naber, P. A., & Van Haeften, T. (2000). Anatomical organization of the parahippocampal–hippocampal network. *Annals of the New York Academy of Sciences*, **911**, 1–24.

Wittling, W. (1995). Brain asymmetry and the control of autonomic physiological activity. In R. J. Davidson & K. Hugdahl (Eds.), *Brain asymmetry* (pp. 305–357). Cambridge, MA: MIT Press.

Wittling, W., & Pfluger, M. (1990). Neuroendocrine hemisphere asymmetries. *Brain and Cognition*, **14**, 243–265.

Woodward, S. A., Lenzenweger, M. F., Kagan, J., Snidman, N. C., & Arcus, D. (2000). Taxonomic structure of infant reactivity. *Psychological Science*, **11**, 300–305.

Wuthnow, R. (2006). *America and the challenges of religious diversity*. Princeton, NJ: Princeton University Press.

Yu, J., & Gracia, J. J. E. (2003). Rationality and happiness: From the ancients to the early Medievals. In J. Yu & J. J. E. Gracia (Eds.), *Rationality and happiness* (pp. 1–16). Rochester, NY: University of Rochester Press.

Zisapel, N. (2001). Melatonin–dopamine interactions: From basic neurochemistry to a clinical setting. *Cell Molecular Neurobiology*, **21**, 605–616.

COMMENTARY

Laurence Steinberg

The study of biological influences on psychological development has a long history among scholars of adolescence (Collins & Steinberg, 2006). This *Monograph* by Kagan, Snidman, Kahn, and Towsley (2007) departs from this tradition in a very important way, however. In the empirical literature on adolescent development, the study of biology is seen mainly in research on the impact of the somatic, hormonal, and, increasingly, neurobiological changes associated with puberty; to most scholars of adolescence, biology is viewed as a change agent (Susman & Rogol, 2004). In the present *Monograph*, though, the emphasis is not on biology as a source of transformation but on biology as a source of stability. Its focus is on the persistence into middle adolescence of biological and psychological differences between individuals that were first observed in infancy. Although there have been prior studies of adolescent manifestations of early temperament—ironically, one of them authored by this commentator (Steinberg, 1985)—it is not a topic that has received a good deal of sustained attention, and certainly no previous investigators have blended such a wide and unusual array of biological and behavioral indicators of temperament in the long-term longitudinal perspective characteristic of this highly original *Monograph*.

The sample studied here is well-known among developmental scientists interested in the biological underpinnings of temperament (Kagan, 1994). Very early in life, a subset of these individuals (20% of the sample) were identified as high-reactive, a group of babies who exhibited high motor activity and frequent crying, and a second subset (40% of the sample) were classified as low-reactive, and showed the opposite profile. These two groups of youngsters who were at the temperamental extremes as infants are the focus of the current report, and the central question posed is whether the biological and behavioral patterns that distinguished these groups at earlier points in development are visible now that the individuals have turned 15. The answer, by and large, is that temperament is preserved for some but not all, in some respects but not others, and, most importantly, more strongly in people's psychological functioning than in their biology.

Although the high- and low-reactive groups do not always differ in predicted ways as teenagers, when they do, the differences are consistent with the notion that their different infant temperaments were preserved, to use the authors' terminology, into adolescence. Many of the highly reactive infants grew up to be what might best be described as "nervous": when interviewed at age 15, compared with their low-reactive peers, they smiled and made spontaneous comments less often and appeared more tense; when they described themselves, they were more likely to say they are morose, that they worry about interpersonal relationships, and they are less likely to report being happy. (These nervous teenagers were also significantly more religious than their peers, but I will resist the temptation to render a causal interpretation of *that* correlation.) However, the evidence for continuity over time is far stronger when behavioral and self-reported indicators are examined than when biological functioning is measured directly. Indeed, across a very extensive battery assessing brain activity and cardiovascular functioning in mid-adolescence, few significant differences were found between those who had been highly reactive as infants and their low-reactive counterparts. Over time, and notably, between ages 11 and 15, biological continuity fades, while behavioral stability is maintained, at least to some modest degree. And, as the authors note, over this interval the connections between contemporaneous biological and behavioral indicators weaken as well.

The fact that biological and behavioral indicators of negative reactivity become increasingly disconnected as individuals mature is not all that surprising. With age, individuals learn how to adapt behaviorally to their biological predilections, and adolescents who are especially aroused by the unfamiliar or unexpected likely become increasingly able to compensate for an easily excitable amygdala with more sophisticated emotion-regulation abilities that are facilitated by the ongoing maturation of brain systems that govern self-control (Steinberg, 2007). This story line leads, however, to the prediction of greater stability over time in biological than in psychological functioning. Why the opposite appears to be true—why behavior is more stable than the biology presumed to undergird it—is the *Monograph*'s big (and unanswered) mystery.

Several possibilities come to mind. One is that the underlying causes of temperamental continuity over time are not primarily biological, but social. Thus the biological predisposition toward negative reactivity that is present early in life, and reflected in heightened motor activity and frequent crying observed during infancy, sets in motion a behavioral trajectory that is self-perpetuating even as the biological systems that originated the behavior may themselves change (see Fox, Hane, & Pine, 2007). Emotionally reactive children often provoke responses from parents and significant others that strengthen their temperamental tendency—parental overprotectiveness makes fearful children more anxious, and the peer rejection that often results in childhood from excessive timidity likely leads to social withdrawal and increased worry about being rebuffed in the future. These consequences, in turn, lead to more overprotectiveness and rejection, which continue the cycle and, in so doing, "preserve" the temperament.

This is not the preservative process implied by the *Monograph*'s authors, however. Kagan and colleagues suggest that the nervous anxiety characteristic of the adolescents who were highly reactive infants stems from their heightened awareness of the visceral sensations generated by a *"permanently* sensitized" amygdala–hippocampal pathway (emphasis added), but this suggestion is undermined by the general absence of over-time continuity in the various measures of brain and cardiovascular functioning, and by the increasingly weak contemporaneous links between biology and behavior observed once individuals reach preadolescence. If the pathways were indeed kindled, as the authors suggest, these longitudinal links should be more impressive than they are, and the contemporaneous links should become stronger, not weaker, over time.

Whence the biological discontinuity, then? A second possibility is that the biological changes of puberty remodel brain systems in ways that undercut the stability in biological functioning seen prepubertally. Our emerging understanding of brain development in adolescence points to the period as one of surprising, experience-dependent plasticity, especially in systems that undergird stress responsivity and the coordination of emotion and cognition (Steinberg, Dahl, Keating, Kupfer, Masten, & Pine, 2006). Indeed, there is good evidence that the hormonal changes of puberty make individuals more sensitive to stress (Walker, Sabuwalla, & Huot, 2004) and to the social environment (Nelson, Leibenluft, McClure, & Pine, 2005), which conceivably could lead to different patterns of neural remodeling among young adolescents who are exposed to highly stressful environments versus those whose environments are supportive. In other words, patterns of neurobiological functioning seen in infancy may be undone by environmental factors present during and around the time of puberty.

Understanding why and under what conditions the transition into adolescence interrupts continuity in biological and, to a lesser degree, psychological functioning is an intriguing question. Unfortunately, however, there is scant attention paid in this *Monograph* to the adolescent experiences of the study participants, which is a significant shortcoming of an otherwise creative and provocative piece of work. The period between 11 and 15 is arguably one of the most, if not *the* most, important transitional periods in the human life span, but it is treated here as if it were any ordinary 4-year interval. The list of changes that regularly take place during these 4 years is absolutely staggering—not only puberty and the concomitant changes it leads to in appearance, affect, and motivation, but the onset of hypothetical thinking, transformations in family relations, the emergence of peer crowds and romantic relationships, the transition to secondary school, and, of course, the remodeling of many brain regions, systems, and circuits, to name just some of the more significant events. G. Stanley Hall's contention that adolescence is "a new birth" (Hall, 1904, p. xiii) may have been an overstatement, but new research on the period, informed by work on brain development and neural plasticity, has led many contemporary scientists to reconsider the field's sweeping dismissal of Hall's view as romantic hyperbole (Dahl & Hariri, 2005).

If patterns of biological and behavioral functioning during adolescence are neither as predictable from the past or as interconnected with each other as they had been in earlier developmental epochs, perhaps the explanation inheres in the nature of the adolescent transition. Although it is important to ask whether extremes of early temperament are preserved into adolescence, it is also important to identify those individuals for whom early biology continues to affect later functioning and those for whom it does not, and to search for the factors that shape their different developmental trajectories. Those factors are likely to inhere in the interaction between the individual's biology and the social context in which the adolescent transition occurs. Being born with an extreme temperament may be destiny, but only if the destination is no longer than 10 years down the road, and even then, only if the contours of the road and the terrain over which it travels remain little changed.

References

Collins, W. A., & Steinberg, L. (2006). Adolescent development in interpersonal context. In N. Eisenberg (Vol. Ed.), W. Damon & R. Lerner (Eds.), *Social, emotional, and personality development. Handbook of Child Psychology* (pp. 1003–1067). New York: Wiley.

Dahl, R., & Hariri, A. (2005). Lessons from G. Stanley Hall: Connecting new research in biological sciences to the study of adolescent development. *Journal of Research on Adolescence*, **15**, 367–382.

Fox, N., Hane, A., & Pine, D. (2007). Plasticity for affective neurocircuitry: How the environment affects gene expression. *Current Directions in Psychological Science*, **16**, 1–5.

Hall, G. S. (1904). *Adolescence*. New York: Appleton.

Kagan, J. (1994). *Galen's Prophecy*. New York: Basic Books.

Kagan, J., Snidman, N., Kahn, V., & Towsley, S. (2007). The preservation of two infant temperaments into adolescence. *SRCD Monographs*, **72**(2).

Nelson, E., Leibenluft, E., McClure, E., & Pine, D. (2005). The social re-orientation of adolescence: A neuroscience perspective on the process and its relation to psychopathology. *Psychological Medicine*, **35**, 163–174.

Steinberg, L. (1985). Early temperamental antecedents of Type A behavior. *Developmental Psychology*, **22**, 1171–1180.

Steinberg, L. (2007). Risk-taking in adolescence: New perspectives from brain and behavioral science. *Current Directions in Psychological Science*, **16**, 55–59.

Steinberg, L., Dahl, R., Keating, D., Kupfer, D., Masten, A., & Pine, D. (2006). Psychopathology in adolescence: Integrating affective neuroscience with the study of context. In D. Cicchetti & D. Cohen (Eds.), *Developmental psychopathology, Vol. 2: Developmental neuroscience* (pp. 710–741). New York: Wiley.

Susman, E., & Rogol, A. (2004). Puberty and psychological development. In R. Lerner & L. Steinberg (Eds.), *Handbook of adolescent psychology* (2nd ed., pp. 15–44). New York: Wiley.

Walker, E. F., Sabuwalla, Z., & Huot, R. (2004). Pubertal neuromaturation, stress sensitivity, and psychopathology. *Development and Psychopathology*, **16**, 807–824.

COMMENTARY

FINISHED AND UNFINISHED BUSINESS

Nathan A. Fox

It may be fair to say that developmental psychologists have had an approach-avoidance conflict towards research on the lasting importance of early-appearing individual differences or of events early in life (including prenatal development) on subsequent psychological development (see Caspi, Harrington, Milne, Amell, Theodore, & Moffitt, 2003). On the one hand, there are the studies of children who have been exposed to neurotoxins in utero demonstrating the lasting effects of such exposure on attention and cognition (Mattson & Riley, 1998; Welsh-Carre, 2005). And there are long-term follow-up studies of infants born with congenital cataracts demonstrating "sleeper effects" in which certain competencies, known to emerge in late childhood, adolescence, or adulthood, are impaired, if the infant is deprived of early visual experience (Maurer, Mondloch, & Lewis, 2007). On the other hand, developmental science is dedicated to the notion that environmental intervention, particularly in the early years of life, can have positive effects upon children who have experienced early adversity (Gottlieb & Blair, 2004). And the area of resilience has focused on identifying factors that are facilitative of adaptive behavior across multiple developmental transitions (Masten, Burt, Roisman, Obradovic, Long, & Tellegen, 2004). Even within the areas of normative or typical development, the power of the transactional model, first articulated by Sameroff (1975), continues to exert an influence on thinking about pathways or trajectories to adaptive and maladaptive outcome. The transactional model states that development occurs within a context, initially, focused on the caregiver–infant interaction, then broadened to the family, and later the peer and school environments. This model is an extension of Bronfenbrenner's ecological model of development (Bronfenbrenner & Ceci, 1994), in which the child is nested within an ever-broadening set of contexts that exert influence on her development. The transactional approach highlights the importance of the child's and context's contributions to these interactions and focuses on the bi-directional influences that each have on the other (Sameroff, 1975, 2000). As all-encompassing as this transactional model is, psychologists have attempted empirically and conceptually to place different weights upon these influences, with some placing emphasis on the child's contribution (Scarr & McCartney, 1983), others more directly on the parents and family (Belsky & Barends, 2002), and still others on the cultural context of development (Rogoff, 1990).

Part of the issue with understanding the effects of early experience is an issue of measurement. We can all understand why exposure in utero to significant qualities of alcohol or neurotoxins such as lead during certain periods of fetal development may increase the likelihood of cognitive deficits in childhood (Chiodo, Jacobson, & Jacobson, 2004). Level of exposure can be measured and the effects on neurogenesis can be quantified. Data describing the neurobiology and embryology of fetal development have elegantly described the timing and sequence of brain development during the prenatal period (see Monk, Webb, & Nelson, 2001, for a review). Exposure to toxins interferes with that development and compromises brain architecture. Hence it is not surprising that such exposure leads to atypical outcomes. It is important to note that variability in outcomes continues to puzzle psychologists, as individual differences in behavioral outcomes appear to be present in children exposed to similar levels of certain neurotoxins at similar points in prenatal life.

It is more difficult to understand why individual differences in temperament in infancy should have a lasting effect on personality and social development. There have been multiple definitions of infant temperament and as many approaches to its measurement. The modern study of infant temperament, articulated by Thomas and Chess (1977) almost 40 years ago, relied for some time on questionnaire methods to identify individual differences in infant temperament. While there is some value to understanding parent or caregiver perception of individual differences in infant disposition, the data from these methods may not directly reflect the biological reality of infant temperament. Of notable exception is the work of Rothbart and her colleagues who developed questionnaire methods for studying infant and child temperament based, in part, on conceptual approaches that involved understanding physiological differences in infant reactivity (Rothbart, Ahadi, Hershey, & Fisher, 2001).

The pioneering work of Jerome Kagan and his colleagues has changed our understanding of the importance of early individual differences in infant reactivity and the link between these differences and social behavioral outcomes (Kagan, Reznick, & Snidman, 1987, 1988; Kagan, Reznick, & Gibbons, 1989). Kagan's work describing a group of children characterized by heightened vigilance for novelty broke new ground for three important reasons. First, most previous research on infant temperament utilized questionnaire methods. For example, a well-done longitudinal study in Australian (Prior, Smart, Sanson, & Oberklaid, 2000) was based initially on questionnaires to parents about their children. Kagan, by contrast, relied on behavioral observation of children in the laboratory to identify those who exhibited the temperament of behavioral inhibition. There are of course those who would argue that questionnaire methods continue to be useful in describing variations in children's temperament (see Rothbart & Bates, 2006, for a full discussion). He then followed these children over time, creating the laboratory situations that allowed him to observe the behaviors conceptually linked to the temperament of behavioral inhibition at successive ages. As such, Kagan and colleagues reported on a fair degree of stability of the trait of behavioral inhibition from infancy through childhood. A second difference in Kagan's approach was his use of extreme, selected samples rather than examining the behavior across a typical population of children. The research from his laboratory examined stability of behavior and physiological correlates of behavioral inhibition amongst children who at least initially present with behaviors that are at the extreme end of the distribution. One of the arguments that Kagan and colleagues have made is that temperament represents a trait and that this trait may be viewed as a category in nature (Kagan, 1994; Kagan, Snidman, & Arcus, 1998). Thus, behaviorally inhibited children, in Kagan's view, are qualitatively different as a result of a confluence of behavioral, biological, and neurochemical elements, which together create this type of child. Although each measure, whether behavioral or physiological, is itself on a continuous scale, the category of behavioral inhibition is the unique set of data from each of these measurements.

The third innovation of Kagan's research and perhaps the one that has had the broadest impact is the link that was made between the research on behavioral inhibition and the work that was itself just emerging at the time, describing the neural circuitry associated with fear. Kagan sensed the implications of the work of Joseph LeDoux (LeDoux, 2000; LeDoux, Iwata, Cicchetti, & Reis, 1988) and Michael Davis, (1986, 1992) in working out, in elegant detail, the neural circuitry underlying conditioned fear. Their work suggested that at the heart of the circuitry that underlay fear responses in the rat was a small structure in the mid-brain called the amygdala. These neuroscientists detailed the different nuclei within the amygdala and their functions with regard to input and output. The central nucleus of the amygdala (Cna) was found to be an important way station from which projections found their way to other limbic centers that controlled heart rate, neuroendocrine responses, and freezing behavior. Input into the amygdala from thalamic, sensory cortical, and hippocampal areas was "organized" in the amygdala to detect novelty and perhaps threat.

Kagan's observations of the freezing behavior of behaviorally inhibited children and his measurement of their physiological responses, including high and low variable heart rate and elevated cortisol, convinced him that the neurobiological "epicenter" of behavioral inhibition was an over-active amygdala. This hypothesis led to two different approaches to the study of behavioral inhibition. In the first, Kagan and colleagues hypothesized that because of output from the amygdala to the periaquaductal gray, infants with an over-active amygdala should display heightened distress and motor reactivity when confronted with unfamiliar auditory and visual stimuli. They developed a battery and coding system to identify infants who displayed extreme reactions of negative affect and motor activity to these stimuli and predicted that this pattern of behavior would be the precursor for behavioral inhibition later in childhood. This prediction has been confirmed particularly in the relations among these patterns of infant reactivity and behavioral inhibition in early childhood (Kagan & Snidman, 2004; Fox, Henderson, Rubin, Calkins, & Schmidt, 2001). The second approach to the study of behavioral inhibition was to examine directly amygdala activation in individuals who were previously characterized with this temperament. Kagan and colleagues (Schwartz, Wright, Shin, Kagan, & Rauch, 2003) using a functional MRI paradigm reported that adults who were previously identified as behaviorally inhibited displayed greater amygdala activation to novel neutral facial expressions compared with non-inhibited individuals. In a replication and extension of this work, Pérez-Edgar Roberson-Nay, Hardin, Poeth, Guyer, Nelson, McClure, Henderson, Fox, Pine, and Ernst (2007) found that adolescents selected at 4 months of age for their reactivity and characterized during childhood as behaviorally inhibited displayed heightened amygdala activation in response to facial expressions of fear and, indeed, showed heightened amygdala activation to happy faces when asked to rate how afraid they were of that face. This study highlighted an important caveat to understanding an individual's response to uncertainty. That is, the context in which a novel stimulus is presented appears critical for eliciting amygdala activation. Across both studies, individuals who displayed behavioral inhibition in childhood exhibited heightened amygdala activation to discrepant events. These differences in amygdala activation were present even after prolonged period of time had elapsed since their previous assessment of behavioral inhibition.

Both animal data and human neuroimaging data support the role of the amygdala in vigilance and attention to uncertainty. Holland and Gallagher (1999) reviewed the animal data illustrating the importance of the amygdala for attention and vigilance. They found that the Cna modulates attention responses as well as changes in activity during fear conditioning. Whalen (1998) reviewed the human neuroimaging data suggesting that the amygdala is involved in increasing vigilance. Whalen suggests that the amygdala is particularly sensitive to uncertainty and ambiguity. Thus, face stimuli that elicit such uncertainty (e.g., fearful as opposed to angry faces) would more likely elicit stronger amygdala activation. The animal data also suggest that there is important circuitry from amygdala to the forebrain that is involved in modulation of attention. These data as a whole appear to indirectly confirm the observations by Kagan on the role of the amygdala in increasing reactivity and vigilant behavior, particularly in situations of ambiguity. Also, the data implicate attention processes in the etiology of psychopathology, particularly anxiety disorders. As Davis and Whalen (2001) write, "pathological anxiety may not be a disorder of fear, but a disorder of vigilance."

The emphasis on assessing responses to uncertainty can be seen in the methods utilized by Kagan, Snidman, Kahn, and Towsley (2007) in their evaluation of adolescents who had been previously characterized as behaviorally inhibited. Their behavioral observation focused on the adolescent's affect and spontaneous conversations with an unfamiliar experimenter, and in particular around topics that might elicit uncertain responses (e.g., religiosity). They report significant associations between temperament, identified and described when infants were 4 months of age, and behaviors and cognitions in adolescence. For example, high-reactive infants appear to smile less, exhibit more motor tension, talk less (particularly high-reactive boys) and critically, express worries about encountering unfamiliar peers, and novel situations. The pattern of these findings in combination with an examination of physiological measures designed to also elicit responses to novelty allow the authors to identify patterns of response, suggesting that over time, individuals with a biological disposition to exhibit heightened vigilance continue to display uncertainty.

It is interesting to note that the theme of interpretation of uncertainty has been one that has occupied much of Kagan's approach to thinking about development. His early work on individual differences examined infant and child responses to novelty (Kagan & Moss, 1962). And his theoretical approach to understanding infant cognition involved portraying the infant as an active solver of discrepancies in the environment. The work in the current *Monograph* integrates that theme into understanding the lives of adolescents whose biology Kagan would argue directs their perceptions and attention to be hyper vigilant about their world.

UNFINISHED BUSINESS

The current *Monograph* provides a capstone on a program of research that continues to have broad influence on our thinking about the effects of temperament and early experience on trajectories of development into adulthood. A number of questions, though, regarding the lives and development of behaviorally inhibited children remain to be answered. First, can we identify the factors that account for the discontinuities as well as the continuities in the expression of behavioral inhibition over time? Second, what is the role of attention processes in the maintenance of behavioral inhibition or in its modification? And third, does the social context of adolescence affect the expression of inhibited behavior and lead to decreased chances for finding continuities across this time period.

Factors Affecting Continuity of Behavioral Inhibition

In a recent review of longitudinal studies that examined and assessed behavioral inhibition, Degnan and Fox (2007) identified several factors that have been proposed as possible contributors to the stability or discontinuity of this behavioral disposition over time. These include styles of parenting, emergence of inhibitory control processes, and biological factors within the child. The data on parenting suggest that certain caregiving styles appear to maintain and even exacerbate the expression of behavioral inhibition over time (c.f. Rubin, Cheah, & Fox, 2001; Degnan, Henderson, Fox, & Rubin, in press). In particular, caregivers exhibiting over-intrusive behaviors have children who display greater continuity over time in behavioral inhibition, compared with those who are less intrusive and provide greater autonomy for their child. Inhibitory control processes also appear to play a role in the maintenance of inhibited behavior. A study by Henderson and Martin (2004) found that behaviorally inhibited children who were less skilled at inhibitory control (as measured in a delay task) were less likely to remain inhibited over time, compared with those who were more skilled at inhibitory control. At first, this appears counter-intuitive as inhibitory control processes have been linked by a number of theorists to adaptive emotion regulation. On the other hand, behaviorally inhibited children in fact may be over-controlled in their responses and such overcontrol thus may limit their flexibility to respond adaptively in social situations. Finally, biological factors were examined in relation to the maintenance of behavioral inhibition. Henderson, Fox, and Rubin (2001) found that temperamentally reactive infants who exhibited right frontal electroencephalogram (EEG) asymmetry were more likely to show heightened behavioral inhibition, whereas infants with this temperament who did not exhibit right frontal EEG asymmetry did not show the heightened behavioral inhibition.

A second within-child factor may be their genetic disposition. A recent paper by Fox, Nichols, Henderson, Rubin, Schmidt, Hamer, Ernst, and Pine (2005) reported that behaviorally inhibited children who were either homozygous or heterozygous for the short allele of the serotonin transport gene and whose mothers reported decreased social support were more likely to show heightened behavioral inhibition over time. Clearly, developmental trajectories are a product of gene–environment interaction. Identifying both the candidate gene and significant activating aspects of the environment needs future research.

The issue of identifying factors leading to continuity or discontinuity takes on an important public health component with regard to the heightened incidence of anxiety disorders among the population of behaviorally inhibited children. This increased incidence has been reported elsewhere (Biederman, Hirshfeld-Becker, Rosenbaum, Herot, Friedman, Snidman, Kagan, & Faraone, 2001) and reviewed in detail (Perez-Edgar & Fox, 2005). Suffice it to say that a significant percentage of behaviorally inhibited children display diagnosed anxiety disorders in the adolescent period. Just who goes on to develop a disorder and who does not is not only of scientific interest but also of clinical relevance.

The Role of Attention in Behavioral Inhibition

Attention, in the form of heightened vigilance to threat, may play a key role in the maintenance of behavioral inhibition. And, attention bias to threat may provide an important link between the neural substrates of behavioral inhibition (e.g., heightened amygdala activation) and prefrontal areas that are involved in the control of orienting and selective attention processes (c.f. Fox, Hane, & Pine, 2007; Bar-Haim, Lamy, Pergamin, Bakermans-Kranenburg, & van IJzendoorn, 2007). Biases in processing threat-related information have been assigned a prominent role in the etiology and maintenance of anxiety disorders, the most common class of psychiatric illness (Mathews & MacLeod, 2002). The attention system of anxious individuals may be biased in favor of threat-related stimuli in the environment. Social threats represent a class of stimuli where particularly robust attention biases emerge, consistent with the powerful influence of social factors on survival. Moreover, work in neuroscience suggests that biases towards social threat and the modulation of vigilance for threat may be associated with the same neural circuits hypothesized to be involved in the expression of behavioral inhibition. Clarifying the cognitive and neural mechanisms underlying the expression of threat-related attention bias to social stimuli in behaviorally inhibited children would therefore seem to be an important research direction.

Continuity of Behavioral Inhibition Into the Adolescent Context and Beyond

Adolescence is an important context for studying the continuity and expression of behavioral inhibition over time. Adolescence brings with it a new set of social demands marked by changes in heterosocial activity (Collins, 2003). The confluence of infant and child temperament and the new social demands of adolescence affect the child's attention bias and physiological reactivity and also directly affect social cognitions and behaviors including friendships, self-concept, and peer relationships (La Greca & Prinstein, 1999). These forces may also influence the development of psychopathology, particularly anxiety disorders in the instance of temperamental inhibition. Adolescence is a period of significant development and transition in which there are changes across multiple domains including the biological, interpersonal, cognitive, and cultural (Grotevant, 1998; Masten, Coatsworth, Neeman, Gest, Tellegen, & Garmezy, 1995). The transitions and changes that occur across these domains mutually influence each other and are driven in part by prior developmental changes in self-perceptions and individual differences in temperament or personality (Grotevant, 1998; Shiner & Caspi, 2003).

During the adolescent years, peer relations and heterosocial activity take on increasing prominence, importance, and complexity. The specific demands of the social context include negotiating romantic relationships and establishing stable mature friendship patterns (Collins, 2003). The adolescent social context is highly dynamic. Less than half of best friendships survive over a year, one-third to one-half of friendship groups break apart over the course of the academic year, and romantic relationships are often measured in weeks (Connolly, Furman, & Konarski, 2000). This is coupled with the social norms that expect the child to engage in these relationships. Thus, adolescence can be a time of near-constant negotiation and renegotiation of social status. This would be stressful for most individuals. For the behaviorally inhibited socially reticent child, this may be of particular concern and cause a good deal of worry and anxiety. Thus, adolescence is a challenge to the attention style and social competence or lack of competence that the behaviorally inhibited child has developed over time. As such, adolescence is a period that has the potential to magnify the effects of early temperamental differences.

An alternative view would find the adolescent period as transformative such that continuities from infancy and childhood in personality may disappear as a result of entry into this developmental period and context. However, temperament biases do not necessarily get transformed during the period of adolescence to the point that these early dispositions are no longer relevant. Indeed, recent work by Caspi et al. (2003) would seem to argue that the strength of continuities from early temperament may in some instances get stronger with time, post-adolescence as individuals enter into adulthood. Reporting on the Dunedin sample, Caspi et al. (2003) found continuities from age 3 temperament to age 26. Temperamentally inhibited children grew up to display, at age 26, greater over control, and nonassertive personalities, reporting that they took little pleasure in life. Indeed, in some instances, Caspi et al. (2003) report that relations between age 3 year temperament and later personality were stronger at age 26 than during adolescence. The authors reason that as individuals leave the adolescent period and enter into adulthood, they also leave the constraints of home environment. They can choose their profession, where they want to live, how interactive or not they wish to be. Thus, the early manifestations of behavioral inhibition and the experiences of childhood may in fact express themselves in an even more dramatic fashion as adolescents enter adulthood.

Acknowledgment

The author would like to thank Daniel Pine and Heather Henderson for their comments and input for this piece.

References

Bar-Haim, Y., Lamy, D., Pergamin, L., Bakermans-Kranenburg, M. J., & van IJzendoorn, M. H. (2007). Threat-related attentional bias in anxious and non-anxious individuals: A meta-analytic study. *Psychological Bulletin*, **133**, 1–24.

Belsky, J., & Barends, N. (2002). Personality and parenting. In M. H. Bornstein (Ed.), *Handbook of parenting: Vol 3, being and becoming a parent* (pp. 415–438). Hillsdale, NJ: Erlbaum.

Biederman, J., Hirshfeld-Becker, D. R., Rosenbaum, J. F., Herot, C., Friedman, D., Snidman, N., Kagan, J., & Faraone, S. V. (2001). Further evidence of association between behavioral inhibition and social anxiety in children. *American Journal of Psychiatry*, **158**, 1673–1679.

Bronfenbrenner, U., & Ceci, S. J. (1994). Nature-nurture reconceptualized in a developmental perspective: A bioecological perspective. *Psychological Review*, **101**, 568–586.

Caspi, A., Harrington, H., Milne, B., Amell, J. W., Theodore, R. F., & Moffitt, T. E. (2003). Children's behavioral styles at age 3 linked to their adult personality traits at age 26. *Journal of Personality*, **71**, 495–513.

Chiodo, L. M., Jacobson, S. W., & Jacobson, J. L. (2004). Neurodevelopmental effects of postnatal lead exposure at very low levels. *Neurotoxicology and Teratology*, **26**, 359–371.

Collins, W. A. (2003). More than a myth: The developmental significance of romantic relationships during adolescence. *Journal of Research on Adolescence*, **13**, 1–24.

Connolly, J., Furman, W., & Konarski, R. (2000). The role of peers in the emergence of heterosexual romantic relationships in adolescence. *Child Development*, **71**, 1395–1408.

Davis, M. (1986). Pharmacological and anatomical analysis of fear conditioning using the fear-potentiated startle paradigm. *Behavioral Neuroscience*, **100**, 814–824.

Davis, M. (1992). The role of the amygdala in fear and anxiety. *Annual Review of Neuroscience*, **15**, 353–375.

Davis, M., & Whalen, P. J. (2001). The amygdala: Vigilance and emotion. *Molecular Psychiatry*, **6**, 13–34.

Degnan, K. A., & Fox, N. A. (2007). Behavioral inhibition and anxiety disorders: Multiple levels of a resilience process. *Development and Psychopathology*, **19**, 729–746.

Degnan, K. A., Henderson, H. A., Fox, N. A., & Rubin, K. H. (in press). Predicting social wariness in middle childhood: The moderating roles of child care history, maternal personality, and maternal behavior. *Social Development*.

Fox, N. A., Hane, A. A., & Pine, D. S. (2007). Plasticity of Affective Neurocircuitry: How the environment affects gene expression. *Current Directions in Psychological Research*, **16**, 1–5.

Fox, N. A., Henderson, H. A., Rubin, K. H., Calkins, S. D., & Schmidt, L. A. (2001). Continuity and discontinuity of behavioral inhibition and exuberance. *Child Development*, **72**, 1–21.

Fox, N. A., Nichols, K. E., Henderson, H. A., Rubin, K. H., Schmidt, L. A., Hamer, D. H., Ernst, M., & Pine, D. S. (2005). Evidence for a Gene Environment Interaction in Predicting Behavioral Inhibition in Middle Childhood. *Psychological Science*, **16**, 921–926.

Gottlieb, G., & Blair, C. (2004). How early experience matters in intellectual development in the case of poverty. *Prevention Science*, **5**, 245–252.

Grotevant, H. D. (1998). Adolescent Development in Family Contexts. In W. Damon (Series Ed.)Eisenberg, N. (Vol. Ed.), *Handbook of child psychology: Vol. 3. Social, emotional and personality development* (5th ed, pp. 1097–1149). New York: Wiley.

Henderson, H. A., Fox, N. A., & Rubin, K. H. (2001). Temperamental contributions to social behavior: The moderating roles of frontal EEG asymmetry and gender. *Journal of the American Academy of Child and Adolescent Psychiatry*, **40**, 68–74.

Henderson, H. A., & Martin, J. (April, 2004). Individual differences in the adaptiveness of self-control. *Paper presented at the biennial meeting of the International Society for Infant Studies*, Chicago IL.

Holland, P. C., & Gallagher, M. (1999). Amygdala circuitry in attentional and representational processes [Review]. *Trends in Cognitive Science*, **3**, 65–73.

Kagan, J. (1994). *Galen's Prophecy*. New York: Basic Books.

Kagan, J., & Moss, H. (1962). *Birth to maturity*. New York: Wiley Press.

Kagan, J., & Snidman, N. (2004). *The long shadow of temperament*. Cambridge, MA: Harvard University Press.

Kagan, J., Snidman, N., & Arcus, D. (1998). Childhood derivatives of high- and low-reactivity in infancy. *Child Development*, **69**, 1483–1493.

Kagan, J., Snidman, N., Kahn, V., & Towsley, S. K. (2007). The preservation of two infant temperaments into adolescence. *Society for Research in Child Development Monographs*, **72**(2).

Kagan, J., Reznick, J. S., & Gibbons, J. (1989). Inhibited and uninhibited types of children. *Child Development*, **60**, 838–845.

Kagan, J., Reznick, J. S., & Snidman, N. (1987). The physiology and psychology of behavioral inhibition in children. *Child Development*, **58**, 1459–1473.

Kagan, J., Reznick, J. S., & Snidman, N. (1988). Biological bases of childhood shyness. *Science*, **240**, 167–171.

La Greca, A. M., & Prinstein, M. J. (1999). The Peer Group. In W. K. Silverman & T. H. Ollendick (Eds.), *Developmental issues in the clinical treatment of children and adolescents* (pp. 171–198). Needham Heights, MA: Allyn and Bacon.

LeDoux, J. E. (2000). Emotion circuits in the brain. *Annual Review of Neuroscience*, **23**, 155–184.

LeDoux, J. E., Iwata, J., Cicchetti, P., & Reis, D. J. (1988). Different projections of the central amygdaloid nucleus mediate autonomic and behavioral correlates of conditioned fear. *Journal of Neuroscience*, **8**, 2517–2529.

Masten, A. S., Burk, K. B., Roisman, G. I., Obradovic, J., Long, J. D., & Tellegen, A. (2004). Resources and resilience in the transition to adulthood: Continuity and change. *Development and Psychopathology*, **16**, 1071–1094.

Masten, A. S., Coatsworth, J. D., Neeman, J., Gest, S. D., Tellegen, A., & Garmezy, N. (1995). The structure and coherence of competence from childhood through adolescence. *Child Development*, **66**, 1635–1659.

Mathews, A., & MacLeod, C. (2002). Induced processing biases have causal effects on anxiety. *Cognition and Emotion*, **16**, 331–354.

Mattson, S. N., & Riley, E. P. (1998). A review of neurobehavioral deficits in children with fetal alcohol syndrome or prenatal exposure to alcohol. *Alcoholism: Clinical and Experimental Research*, **22**, 279–294.

Maurer, D., Mondloch, C. J., & Lewis, T. L. (2007). Sleeper effects. *Developmental Science*, **10**, 40–47.

Monk, C. S., Webb, S. J., & Nelson, C. A. (2001). Prenatal neurobiological development: Molecular mechanisms and anatomical change. *Developmental Neuropsychology*, **19**, 211–236.

Perez-Edgar, K. E., & Fox, N. A. (2005). Temperament and anxiety disorders. *Child and Adolescent Psychiatric Clinics of North America*, **14**, 681–706.

Pérez-Edgar, K., Roberson-Nay, R., Hardin, M. G., Poeth, K., Guyer, A. E., Nelson, E. E., McClure, E. B., Henderson, H. A., Fox, N. A., Pine, D. S., & Ernst, M. (2007). Attention alters neural responses to evocative faces in behaviorally inhibited adolescents. *Neuroimage*, **35**, 1536–1548.

Prior, M., Smart, D., Sanson, A., & Oberklaid, F. (2000). Does shy-inhibited temperament in childhood lead to anxiety problems in adolescence? *Journal of the American Academy of Child and Adolescent Psychiatry*, **39**, 461–468.

Rogoff, B. (1990). *Apprenticeship in thinking: Cognitive development in social context*. New York: Oxford University Press.

Rothbart, M. K., Ahadi, S. A., Hershey, K. L., & Fischer, P. (2001). Investigations of temperament from three to seven years: The children's behavior questionnaire. *Child Development*, **72**, 1394–1408.

Rothbart, M. K., & Bates, J. E. (2006). Temperament. In W. Damon, R. M. Lerner & N. Eisenberg (Ed.), *Handbook of child psychology: Vol. 3, Social, emotional, and personality development* (pp. 99–166). New York: Wiley.

Rubin, K. H., Cheah, C. S. L., & Fox, N. A. (2001). Emotion regulation, parenting, and display of social reticence in preschoolers. *Early Education and Development*, **12**, 97–115.

Sameroff, A. J. (1975). Transactional models in early social relations. *Human Development*, **18**, 65–79.

Sameroff, A. J. (2000). Developmental systems and psychopathology. *Development and Psychopathology*, **12**, 297–312.

Sanson, A., Pedlow, R., Cann, W., Prior, & Oberklaid, F. (1996). Shyness ratings: Stability and correlates in early childhood. *International Journal of Behavioral Development*, **19**, 705–724.

Scarr, S., & McCartney, K. (1983). How people make their own environments: A theory of genotype-environmental effects. *Child Development*, **54**, 424–435.

Schwartz, C. E., Wright, C. I., Shin, L. M., Kagan, J., & Rauch, S. L. (2003). Inhibited and uninhibited infants "grown up": Adult amygdalar response to novelty. *Science*, **300**, 1952–1953.

Shiner, R., & Caspi, A. (2003). Personality differences in childhood and adolescence: Measurement, development, and consequences. *Journal of Child Psychology and Psychiatry*, **44**, 2–32.

Thomas, A., & Chess, S. (1977). *Temperament and development*. New York: Brunner.

Welch-Carre, E. (2005). The neurodevelopmental consequences of prenatal alcohol exposure. *Advances in Neonatal Care*, **5**, 217–229.

Whalen, P. J. (1998). Fear, vigilance, and ambiguity: Initial human neuroimaging studies of the human amygdala. *Current Directions in Psychological Science*, **7**, 177–188.

CONTRIBUTORS

Nathan A. Fox is Professor of Human Development at the University of Maryland College Park. His area of research interest is in social and emotional development of infants and young children. He has developed methods for assessing brain activity in infants and young children during tasks designed to elicit a range of emotions. His work is funded by the National Institutes of Health and includes a MERIT award. He currently serves on the Biobehavioral Sciences standing review panel for NICHD. Dr. Fox was awarded the Distinguished Scholar Teacher award from the University of Maryland in 2005.

Laurence Steinberg (Ph.D., 1977, Cornell University) is the Distinguished University Professor and Laura H. Carnell Professor of Psychology at Temple University. His research focuses on biological and contextual influences on normative and atypical development during adolescence, most recently, on the connections between brain maturation and adolescent risk-taking.

Jerome Kagan (Ph.D., Yale University) is professor of psychology emeritus at Harvard University, Cambridge, Massachusetts. He is the author of *Galen's Prophecy* (1984), *Three Seductive Ideas* (2002), *An Argument for Mind* (2006), and with Nancy Snidman of *The Long Shadow of Temperament* (2004). His interests include infant temperament, cognitive development and emotional processes.

Nancy Snidman (Ph.D., University of California, Los Angeles) is the EEG Research Director of TRANSCEND (Treatment, Research And Neuro-SCience Evaluation of Neurodevelopmental Disorders) at Massachusetts General Hospital. She is author with Jerome Kagan of *The Long Shadow of Temperament* (2004). Her interests include biological correlates of temperament and individual differences, autism and cognitive development.

Sara Towsley received her B.A. from Tufts University (2005) in clinical psychology and her M.A. in psychology from Brandeis University (2007). She is currently a research associate in the psychology department at Brandeis University.

Vali Kahn received her B.A. from Bryn Mawr (1998) in psychology. She is currently a graduate student in clinical psychology at University of Massachusetts at Boston.

STATEMENT OF EDITORIAL POLICY

The *Monographs* series aims to publish major reports of developmental research that generate authoritative new findings and uses these to foster a fresh perspective or integration of findings on some conceptually significant issue. Submissions from programmatic research projects are welcomed; these may consist of individually or group-authored reports of findings from a single large-scale investigation or from a sequence of experiments centering on a particular question. Multiauthored sets of independent studies that center on the same underlying question may also be appropriate; a critical requirement in such instances is that the various authors address common issues and that the contribution arising from the set as a whole be unique, substantial, and well-integrated. Manuscripts reporting interdisciplinary or multidisciplinary research on significant developmental questions and those including evidence from diverse cultural, racial, ethnic, national, or other contexts are of particular interest. Because the aim of the series is not only to advance knowledge on specialized topics but also to enhance cross-fertilization among disciplines or subfields, the links between the specific issues under study and larger questions relating to developmental processes should emerge clearly for both general readers and specialists on the topic. In short, irrespective of how it may be framed, work that contributes significant data or extends developmental thinking will be considered.

Potential authors are not required to be members of the Society for Research in Child Development or affiliated with the academic discipline of psychology to submit a manuscript for consideration by the *Monographs*. The significance of the work in extending developmental theory and in contributing new empirical information is the crucial consideration.

Submissions should contain a minimum of 80 manuscript pages (including tables and references). The upper boundary of 150–175 pages is more flexible, but authors should try to keep within this limit. Please submit manuscripts electronically to the SRCD Monographs Online Submissions and Review Site (MONOSubmit) at www.srcd.org/monosubmit. Please contact the Monographs office with any questions at monographs@srcd.org.

The corresponding author for any manuscript must, in the submission letter, warrant that all coauthors are in agreement with the content of the manuscript. The corresponding author also is responsible for informing all coauthors, in a timely manner, of manuscript submission, editorial decisions, reviews received, and any revisions recommended. Before publication, the corresponding author must warrant in the submissions letter that the study was conducted according to the ethical guidelines of the Society for Research in Child Development.

Potential authors who may be unsure whether the manuscript they are planning would make an appropriate submission are invited to draft an outline of what they propose and send it to the editor for assessment. This mechanism, as well as a more detailed description of all editorial policies, evaluation processes, and format requirements, is given in the "Guidelines for the Preparation of Publication Submissions," which can be found at the SRCD website by clicking on *Monographs*, or by contacting the editor, W. Andrew Collins, Institute of Child Development, University of Minnesota, 51 E. River Road, Minneapolis, MN 55455-0345; e-mail: wcollins@umn.edu.

Monographs of the Society for Research in Child Development (ISSN 0037-976X), one of three publications of the Society for Research in Child Development, is published three times a year by Blackwell Publishing with offices at 350 Main St., Malden, MA 02148; PO Box 1354, Garsington Rd., Oxford, OX4 2DQ, UK; and PO Box 378 Carlton South, 3053 Victoria, Australia. A subscription to *Monographs of the SRCD* comes with a subscription to *Child Development* (published bimonthly).

INFORMATION FOR SUBSCRIBERS For new orders, renewals, sample copy requests, claims, changes of address, and all other subscription correspondences, please contact the Journals Department at your nearest Blackwell office (address details listed above). UK office phone: +44 (0) 1865-778315; Fax: +44 (0) 1865-471775; Email: customerservices@bos.blackwellpublishing.com; US office phone: 800-835-6770 or 781-388-8206; Fax: 781-388-8232; Email: customerservices@blackwellpublishing.com; Asia office phone: +65 6511 8000; Fax: +44 (0) 1865-471775; Email: customerservices@blackwellpublishing.com.

INSTITUTIONAL PREMIUM RATES* FOR MONOGRAPHS OF THE SRCD/CHILD DEVELOPMENT 2007 The Americas $543; Rest of World £386. Customers in Canada should add 6% GST to The Americas price or provide evidence of entitlement to exemption. Customers in the UK or EU should add VAT at 6% or provide a VAT registration number or evidence of entitlement to exemption

*A Premium Institutional Subscription includes online access to full text articles from 1997 to present, where available. Print and online-only rates are also available.

BACK ISSUES Back issues are available from the publisher at the current single issue rate.

MICROFORM The journal is available on microfilm. For microfilm service, address inquiries to ProQuest Information and Learning, 300 North Zeeb Rd., Ann Arbor, MI 48106-1346, USA. Bell and Howell Serials Customer Service Department (800) 521-0600 ×2873.

MAILING Periodical postage paid at Boston, MA and additional offices. Mailing to the rest of the world by International Mail Express. Canadian mail is sent by Canadian publications mail agreement number 40573520. Postmaster: Send all address changes to *Monographs of the Society for Research in Child Development*, Blackwell Publishing Inc., Journals Subscription Department, 350 Main St., Malden, MA 02148-5020.

Blackwell Synergy Sign up to receive *Blackwell Synergy* free email alerts with complete *Monographs of the SRCD* tables of contents and quick links to article abstracts from the most current issue. Simply go to www.blackwell-synergy.com, select the journal from the list of journals, and click on "Sign-up" for FREE email table of contents alerts.

COPYRIGHT AND PHOTOCOPYING © 2007 Society for Research in Child Development, Inc. All rights reserved. No part of this publication may be reproduced, stored or transmitted in any form or by any means without the prior permission in writing from the copyright holder. Authorization to photocopy items for internal and personal use is granted by the copyright holder for libraries and other users registered with their local Reproduction Rights Organization (RRO), e.g., Copyright Clearance Center (CCC), 222 Rosewood Drive, Danvers, MA 01923, USA (www.copyright.com), provided the appropriate fee is paid directly to the RRO. This consent does not extend to other kinds of copying such as copying for general distribution, for advertising or promotional purposes, for creating new collective works or for resale. Special requests should be addressed to Blackwell Publishing at: journalsrights@oxon.blackwellpublishing.com.

© 2007 Society for Research in Child Development

CURRENT

The Preservation of Two Infant Temperaments Into Adolescence—*Jerome Kagan, Nancy Snidman, Vali Kahn, and Sara Towsley* (SERIAL NO. 287, 2007)

Children's Questions: A Mechanism for Cognitive Development—*Michelle M. Chouinard* (SERIAL NO. 286, 2007)

Best Practices in Quantitative Methods for Developmentalists—*Kathleen McCartney, Margaret R. Burchinal, and Kristen L. Bub* (SERIAL NO. 285, 2006)

Foundations for Self-Awareness: An Exploration through Autism—*R. Peter Hobson, Gayathri Chidambi, Anthony Lee, and Jessica Meyer* (SERIAL NO. 284, 2006)

Our Children Too: A History of the First 25 years of the Black Caucus of the Society for Reserach in Child Development, 1973–1997—*Diana T. Slaughter-Defoe, Aline M. Garrett, Algea O. Harrison-Hale* (SERIAL NO. 283, 2006)

Parental Support, Psychological Control, and Behavioral Control: Assessing Relevance across Time, Culture, and Method—*Brian K. Barber, Heidi E. Stolz, and Joseph A. Olsen* (SERIAL NO. 282, 2005)

Being Hurt and Hurting Others: Children's Narrative Accounts and Moral Judgments of Their Own Interpersonal Conflicts—*Cecilia Wainryb, Beverly A. Brehl, and Sonia Matwin* (SERIAL NO. 281, 2005)

Childhood Sexual Assault Victims: Long-Term Outcomes after Testifying in Criminal Court—*Jodi A. Quas, Gail S. Goodman, Simona Ghetti, Kristen W. Alexander, Robin Edelstein, Allison D. Redlich, Ingrid M. Cordon, and David P. H. Jones* (SERIAL NO. 280, 2005)

The Emergence of Social Cognition in Three Young Chimpanzees—*Michael Tomasello, and Malinda Carpenter* (SERIAL NO. 279, 2005)

Trajectories of Physical Aggression From Toddlerhood to Middle Childhood: Predictors, Correlates, and Outcomes—*NICHD Early Child Care Research Network* (SERIAL NO. 278, 2004)

Constraints on Conceptual Development: A Case Study of the Acquisition of Folkbiological and Folksociological Knowledge in Madagascar—*Rita Astuti, Gregg E. A. Solomon, and Susan Carey* (SERIAL NO. 277, 2004)

Origins and Early Development of Human Body Knowledge—*Virginia Slaughter and Michelle Heron in Collaboration with Linda Jenkins, and Elizabeth Tilse* (SERIAL NO. 276, 2004)

Mother-Child Conversations about Gender: Understanding the Acquisition of Essentialist Beliefs—*Susan A. Gelman, Marrianne Taylor, and Simone Nguyen* (SERIAL NO. 275, 2004)

The Development of Executive Function in Early Childhood—*Philip David Zelazo, Ulrich Müller, Douglas Frye, and Stuart Marcovitch* (SERIAL NO. 274, 2003)

Personal Persistence, Identity Development, and Suicide: A Study of Native and Non-Native North American Adolescents—*Michael J. Chandler, Christopher E. Lalonde, Bryan W. Sokol, and Darcy Hallett* (SERIAL NO. 273, 2003)

Personality and Development in Childhood: A Person-Centered Approach—*Daniel Hart, Robert Atkins, and Suzanne Fegley* (SERIAL NO. 272, 2003)

How Children and Adolescents Evaluate Gender and Racial Exclusion—*Melanie Killen, Jennie Lee-Kim, Heidi McGlothlin, and Charles Stangor* (SERIAL NO. 271, 2002)

Child Emotional Security and Interparental Conflict—*Patrick T. Davies, Gordon T. Harold, Marcie C. Goeke-Morey, and E. Mark Cummings* (SERIAL NO. 270, 2002)

The Developmental Course of Gender Differentiation: Conceptualizing, Measuring and Evaluating Constructs and Pathways—*Lynn S. Liben and Rebecca S. Bigler* (SERIAL NO. 269, 2002)

The Development of Mental Processing: Efficiency, Working Memory, and Thinking—*Andreas Demetriou, Constantinos Christou, George Spanoudis, and Maria Platsidou* (SERIAL NO. 268, 2002)